What's being said about You?

Strategies for Businesses to Monitor Online Reputation.

Ronke Jegede

Copyright

Published by: JIL Publishing, London, UK

ISBN: 978-0-9934509-2-1

First Edition Printed in UK

Table of Contents

Introduction

Reputation is of huge significance to organisations and will always be no matter what kind of organisation it is, be it a small business, big corporation or Non-profit. Good reputation is essential for such organisations to stay competitive and achieve their goals.

Reputations are complicated and are derived from the people or organisations they describe. Reputations differentiate and set organisations and people apart.
A number of notable people, made some profound remarks about reputation which are worthy of note and they are as follows:-

Warren Buffett, is an American business magnate, investor, philanthropist and one of the richest men in the world.

"It takes 20 years to build a reputation and five minutes to ruin it. If you think about that, you'll do things differently."

"We can afford to lose money — even a lot of money. But we can't afford to lose reputation — even a shred of reputation."

"If you lose dollars for the firm by bad decisions, I will be very understanding. If you lose reputation for the firm, I will be ruthless."
- Warren Buffett

Abraham Lincoln was the 16th President of the United States and considered to be of one of "the top 10 most influential presidents".

"Character is like a tree and reputation like its shadow. The shadow is what we think of it; the tree is the real thing."
- Abraham Lincoln

Rupert Murdoch is the owner of some of the most popular newspapers in the world. He was described by Forbes Magazine as "arguably the world's most powerful media tycoon" [1]

"Our reputation is more important than the last hundred million dollars."
- Rupert Murdoch

Sir Richard Branson, is an English business magnate, investor and philanthropist. He is the founder of Virgin Group, which encompasses more than 400 companies.

"Your brand name is only as good as your reputation." - Richard Branson

Jeff Bezos is an American entrepreneur; he is the founder and chief executive officer of Amazon.com. Amazon is probably the largest Internet-based retailer in the United States of America.

"A brand for a company is like a reputation for a person. You earn reputation by trying to do hard things well." - Jeff Bezos

Socrates was a classical Greek (Athenian) philosopher credited as one of the founders of Western philosophy.

"The way to gain good reputation is to endeavor to be what you desire to appear." - Socrates

Henry Ford was one of America's foremost industrialists and the founder of the Ford Motor Company.

"You can't build a reputation on what you are going to do." - Henry Ford

Benjamin Franklin is best known as one of the Founding Fathers who drafted the Declaration of Independence and the Constitution of the United States. [2]

"Glass, china, and reputation are easily cracked, and never mended well".

"It takes many good deeds to build a good reputation, and only one bad one to lose it". - Benjamin Franklin

Dwight L. Moody was an American evangelist and publisher.

"If I take care of my character, my reputation will take care of me". - Dwight L. Moody

Reference

[1] http://www.forbes.com/profile/rupert-murdoch/
[2] http://www.biography.com/people/benjamin-franklin-9301234

Defining Reputation

There are a number of definitions for reputation, some have been listed below:
According to Merriam-Webster's Dictionary, REPUTATION is "the common opinion that people have about someone or something: the way in which people think of someone.

Meanwhile dictionary.law.com defines REPUTATION as "a person's good name, honor or what the community thinks of him/her". [1]

Blacks' Law Dictionary further asserts that "REPUTATION is "a person's credit, honor, character, good name." [2]

Webster's New World Dictionary defines reputation as "estimation in which a person or thing is commonly held, whether favorable or not; character in the view of the public, the community, etc.; repute." [3]

An article in the Business Europe journal states that "[Corporate] Reputation is a valuable and tangible asset." [4].

Bromley extends this definition and describes it as being "both a product (a tangible effect) and a process (in time)." [5].

Furthermore, Coombs and Holladay, assert that "reputations are widely recognized as a valuable, intangible asset." [6]

Charles Fombrun (1996) [7] claims that reputation is created in a premeditated method by organisations taking necessary notice of the setting in which they function.

References

[1] http://dictionary.law.com/Default.aspx?selected=1805
[2] http://thelawdictionary.org/reputation/
[3] http://www.yourdictionary.com/reputation#websters
[4]. Reputations at stake (2000) In Business Europe, p. 2
[5]. Cf. Bromley, D. (2001) Relationships between personal and corporate reputation, p. 320
[6] Coombs W. T., Holladay S. J. (2006) Unpacking the halo effect: reputation and crisis management, p. 123
[7] Fombrun, C. J. (1996). Reputation: Realizing value from corporate image, Harvard Business School, Cambridge, MA.

What is Online Reputation Management (ORM)?

Reputation is extremely important and actually means everything, incurring a negative one can pose an enormous problem in business. This is why reputation management is so essential, because it can help safeguard this invaluable asset.

Online reputation management is basically making certain that you know what is happening to your brand, how it looks online and what is being said about you, whether bad or good. It is the process of improving or repairing your brand/name and its good standing. Reputation management entails constantly monitoring the name of an individual, brand or company, dealing with any issues that pose any threat of damage to it.

Online reputation management or ORM as it is known is the process of enhancing people and businesses so that they look their best online. This can be done by refuting, diminishing or removing the adverse material that can be found on the Internet – overcoming it with more positive material in order to increase the level of your credibility and improve your customers' trust in you.

Online reputation management comprises of managing the search engine results and shielding your company's reputation from harmful online exposure. This is very vital because business decisions are heavily swayed by what is discovered on the web. Basically, an ORM strategy incorporates traditional marketing and public relations with search engine promotion. The ultimate objectives are prominence on search engines and high rankings for positive publicity which will in push negative publicity from the first few pages of the search engine listings and out of public sight. Online searchers seldom look beyond the first two pages of search engine results.

Online reputation management facilitates the management and protection of a company's reputation and also repairing any such damage to reputation by negative publicity online.

Online reputation management is important for businesses of any size. It is about building a positive online presence so that people trust you and want to engage with you. Having a good online reputation is critical because it does not matter how great your products are if people do not trust you, they will not be interested in them.
One thing is clear and unmistakable, a good online reputation does not occur by chance.

Online reputation management includes a diverse number of approaches, focused on monitoring and promoting organisations across multiple online sites which include social media such as:

Social networking sites – Posting content on Facebook, Twitter, MySpace.com, LinkedIn, Pinterest, Google Plus+ and so on.

Customer reviews – Monitoring and responding appropriately to reviews on review sites.

Blogging – Blogging relevantly and updating content regularly be it daily, weekly or monthly with regular content.

Directory listings – Getting website listed in directories employing optimised keywords and categories.

Online PR – Building links, using banners and syndicated article writing.

It is essential that every organisation has a well-defined reputation management strategy which is unique to each business.

Reasons for ORM for Businesses

There are a number of reasons why it is vital for businesses to monitor their online reputation and the following are some of the reasons:-

1. Potential customers will "Google your business" before they buy from you.

The first thing an average person does these days is go online to get some information about what they want to purchase and who they want to purchase from. They will go to Google type in the business name, read the reviews and other relevant information about that business.

2. People only buy from companies that they trust.

When your company has a good online reputation, it portrays your company in a good light and goes a long way in helping build the trust of people. On the other hand, bad reviews will have the opposite effect and drive them into the arms of your competition. Having no reputation at all online can also have the same effect as having adverse online reputation.

3. People do pay attention to what others are saying online

Your online reputation is more pertinent now than ever as customers and potential customers are heeding to the voices of their family, friends, acquaintances and the general public – not just your online postings and advertisements.

What an organisation and other people post online are of paramount significance. Individuals could forget about them but social media tend never to forget!

3. Building your reputation helps with raising brand awareness.

It is easier to build brand awareness when you build your online reputation using different social media platforms, blogs, YouTube videos and the like. It is however essential to do it right because if you do it wrong you will unintentionally harm your reputation online.

4. You gain a competitive advantage with a good reputation.

Having a positive online reputation contributes immensely to the amount of clout and authority you have this causes you to tower above your competitors. The strategy to adopt is to build such great content online such that whenever people search for your company, brand or product, not only do you appear in the first pages of the search results but that you appear in an excellent way. This will inevitably give you an enormous edge over your competition who are either still struggling to position themselves on the first pages of the search results or already have an online presence but their reputation is tarnished online.

5. Online marketing and social media has radically changed the way we do business.

A higher percentage than ever before is being done online and so there is a great surge in the impact of online marketing and social media on our business methods. Online marketing and social media is a strong force that no business can afford to ignore otherwise that business will be completely wiped out.

6. Customers are interested in your values.

Once upon a time what most companies were solely concerned with was their bottom line without any consideration for their reputation. However, things have since changed. Your customers and potential customers do care about the ethics and values of the companies they do business with. If your ethics and values don't meet their expectations, they will simply move on to any competitor who measures up. This will obviously lose your money.

7. Unprincipled competitors may attack your reputation.
Some people are unscrupulous and will stop at nothing to bring their competition down and one of the easiest ways of doing that nowadays is by posting negative reviews online about their competitors. You will be instantly alerted to such attacks when you have a system in place to constantly monitor and improve your online reputation. It is however imperative that you respond to such attacks in the right way, so that you can end up turning it to your benefit.

8. Every action taken online matters.
It is important to understand that every action you take counts, this can either be in your favour or against you as those actions will be scrutinised whether you like it or not. It is therefore vital that you seriously consider the ramifications of anything that you want to post online before you do. Even the way you respond to a nasty customer who obviously deserves a piece of your mind is crucial. You must constantly be thinking of how you can turn even something like that around for good as opposed to responding in a way that will land you in a worse position. Bottom line is that, it doesn't matter who is wrong, what truly counts, is how people perceive you.

9. Your customers' decisions are swayed by what they find out about you online.
The one thing to bear in mind is that before someone purchases something from you, they are almost bound to check your online reputation first and if they are not impressed by what they read about you, they will not buy from you. One

negative posting or review about you in any of the social media channels can make it that much tougher for you to get another customer to buy your products. Such comments also tend to go viral really quickly. A good reputation reassures customers and helps persuade them to buy products and services.

Research shows the following:-

A high proportion of consumers trust online reviews as much as personal recommendations.

A great percentage of consumers do not purchase products with negative online reviews.

A large number of consumers check online reviews before making purchases and are strongly influenced to buy when they read good online reviews.

10. Your competitors are building their profiles

It is important to remember that your company/organisation is not the only one offering your service or products; you have competitors in the same field. One of the obvious ways of generating business is by ensuring that you stand out and showcase yourself poles apart from them in a positive way. What is being said about your organisation is therefore of paramount importance. It is not just about your products or services; it is so much more than that. The way you are perceived online is what sums up your reputation in the market place and this plays a significant role in determining the success or failure of your organisation. Your potential customers choose whether they come to you or take their business to your competition based on your online reputation.

11. A good reputation creates value for companies as stakeholders are strongly influenced by your reputation.

a. Suppliers are more disposed to do business with a company with a positive reputation than one that lacks it.

b. Excellent employees are attracted to your company and employee turnover is low when a company enjoys a good reputation.

c. Investors are more interested in investing in a company with a good reputation.

Here are some common internet search facts you should know about:

- 95% of internet users do not search past the first page of search engine results.
- 80% of people in the Western World researches a product on the internet before purchasing.
- 72% of those that research will not buy if there's a negative comment

Below are some Google search results for Spas:

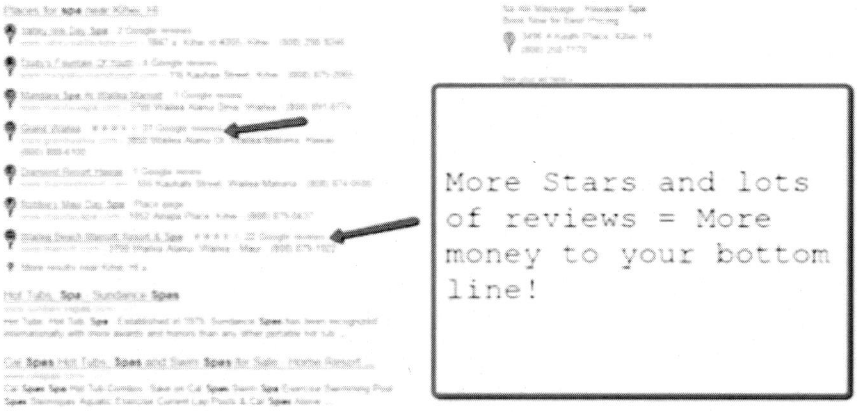

If you were conducting this search, which one of the spas in the search results above would you consider doing business with?

Absolutely! It will obviously be the business with the most reviews and stars. This goes to show how much of an impact your business' online reputation can have on your bottom line.

Monitoring your online reputation must be a non-negotiable action that must be taken if you want your business to survive in this day and age.

Goals of ORM.

There are three main goals of online reputation management and they are as follows:-

1. To build a positive online reputation. This is to do with establishing the reputation of a business. The business could either be a brand new one that has not had the chance to build a reputation for itself or it could be an old one that has no online presence at all and therefore a non-existent reputation. This process involves outlining the culture of the business and setting out clearly what the organisation wants to be known for. It is about setting standards and portraying the company the way they want to be seen both offline and online.

For instance, if a potential customer searches for information online about a company but finds little or nothing —minimal Facebook or Twitter activity, non-existent blog posts or articles— it is highly likely that the potential customer will move on to a competitor because they perceive that the company with little online presence is not the expert in that field. In this instance, producing content and engaging on social media establishes their web presence and demonstrates that they are an authority. This consequently builds trust and aids in converting prospects to customers.

Building a reputation is critical to the survival of any organisation.

2. Maintenance of reputation – This process involves maintaining a company's good image. The fact that a company has already established a great reputation does

not mean that the job is done as anything can happen really to tarnish the reputation. Steps must therefore be actively taken to maintain reputation otherwise the company constantly stands at risk of having its reputation damaged.

The aim is to eliminate or suppress any negative content that is posted online which shows up especially on the first page of Google. If such negative contents are left online, they will eventually tarnish and damage the reputation of the company in question.

Maintenance of reputation is crucial to the continued existence of any organisation.

3. Recovery of reputation – This procedure entails salvaging and repairing the damaged reputation of a company. It is in the best interest of every organisation to put the first two steps into practice and avoid getting to this stage. Loss of reputation can lead to disastrous consequences such as loss of valued customers, loss of loyal staff loss of income etc. However, recovery of reputation process can be embarked upon if an organisation's reputation has been tarnished or damaged for any reason.

Recovery of reputation is the ultimate step to that needs to be taken to rescue an organisation from its demise. It is the step necessary to bring the organisation back from life support.

The Most Common Online Reputation Problems

Frankly, there are a number of issues that can adversely affect your organisations' online reputation. However some of the most prevalent ones are listed below:

Scandals or salacious stories involving your company: if your company has been involved in a scandal (tax fraud, customer disputes, etc.) even if it happened years ago and when the company was under different ownership, it could still be lurking out in cyberspace, and it could be potentially damaging for your company.

1. Your reputation can be smeared by online postings started by vindictive ex-employees, who feel that they have been unfairly dismissed or had to leave unreasonably. They could leave nasty reviews on review sites, post negative comments on social media platforms such as Twitter or Facebook or even start a blog or website to air their negative posts. It takes next to nothing for them to do this and such people usually have strong enough motives and passion to do just this. These types of negative postings or hates can cause reputational damage so don't ignore it, act swiftly to get the posts deleted or the sites removed.

2. Your reputation can be destroyed by online postings started by disgruntled customers who were not satisfied with your services or products. It usually takes one unhappy customer to start something off and if you are not careful if there are other dissatisfied customers that you haven't responded to their complaints, they join in and this take on a snowball effect. They could leave nasty reviews on review sites, post negative comments on social media platforms such as Twitter of

Facebook or even start blogs or websites to vent their negative experiences. You need to respond promptly to complaints about your services or products otherwise you will find that the voices of a crowd are louder than one and the damage can be almost irreparable.

3. Your reputation can be destroyed by online postings started by an antagonistic competitor. They could leave nasty reviews on review sites, post negative comments on social media platforms such as Twitter of Facebook or even start a blog or website to malign your company in order to destroy your business and divert your customers to them. You need to deal with this quickly by tracing the perpetrators and asking them to remove such posts or remove such websites and even threaten legal action or even if commence legal action against them.

4. Your reputation can be ruined by complaints left by consumers on complaint sites, these sites are unlike hate sites as they are not set up by individuals who just have it in for you, be they dissatisfied customers, disgruntled, ex-employees or nasty competitors. Rather they are sites specifically set up where consumers can leave reviews and testimonials about their experiences with businesses, these may be sites like the Better Business Bureau, Consumer Affairs or Angie's List. Sites like these tend to rank very highly and can be difficult to push down, ensure that you handle complaints quickly to avoid them being left in such sites.

5. Your reputation can be wrecked by negative press about your company. When something is news in the papers it is bound to be published online and that is where the tendency to for it to go viral, grow bigger and be everywhere. This piece of

news can is likely to follow your company everywhere it goes. Negative press should be avoided like the plague.

6. Your reputation can be crushed by lies and false information published about your company, all it takes is for one person to set it off and like wildfire it spreads easing. Bad news always tends to travel faster than good news. This can become a big deal so find the source of this fire and douse it fast.

7. Your reputation can be sabotaged by negative reviews posted by discontented customers either on social media sites or review sites such as Yelp, TripAdvisor etc. These popular review sites rank highly on search engine sites such as Google, Bing etc. It is therefore imperative to monitor your reputation online so you can deal with issues like this.

8. Non-existent online presence or an inadequately managed online presence can actually be just as damaging as a negative one. Imagine some potential customers who are contemplating which company to buy from out of yours and two others. The first company they look up on the search engines comes up with negative reviews, of course they will discard the thought of buying from that company, they look up yours and there is neither good or bad reviews online about your company and they look up the third company and it has a strong online presence with a number of good reviews about their products and service. Who do you think will get the custom of these potential customers? You guessed right the company with good reviews. Every company needs a great social media profile online in order to compete otherwise they will lose business.

9. The opinion of influential people and experts in your field is really important, if you do not earn their respect, they could easily say something derogatory about you that will give you

adverse publicity. This might sway potential customers who might believe such comments when they come across them.

10. Lack of diligence about monitoring for damaging comments and pictures on social media sites, search engines, forums and blogs can lead to your reputation being destroyed. Monitoring will keep you well ahead and enable you to nip potential disasters in the bud before they blow to become catastrophic.

Misconceptions about Online Reputation

There are numerous misconceptions about online reputation; some of the most common ones are listed below:

1. A lack of online presence is better than having a negative one. This is basically not true. When a company or individual has no internet presence, it gives the impression that they are out of the loop, not current with what is going on, not to be trusted, bogus and arouses suspicion as to whether the business or person is authentic or not. When a prospective searches for you online and all that is available for them to see are directory listings they may be alarmed about the legitimacy of the company or person who providing the products or services. There are numerous scams on the internet today so customers are more cautious than ever before.

In addition, not having an online presence makes a company seem as if they are still living in the past. In this internet era, it is virtually unheard of that an organisation has no web or social media presence at all. This is a great disadvantage to the company as it is awkward for potential customers to make contact with that person or company and difficult to access useful information online that will help convert that person to being a customer. More so, it also makes the person or company susceptible to imminent attack. One of the advantages of possessing your online estate is that it helps create a defence against negative materials showing up on search engine results.

2. An individual or company should only use Online Reputation Management tools and resources when they are facing a reputation disaster – for instance, when harmful reviews have been posted online about the individual. This is a major error. The reality is that there is much more to online reputation management than this. Online reputation management essentially involves amongst other things ensuring that your reputation is untarnished or not and can endure impending attacks and that your company not only survives such occurrences but also sail through regardless of the issue.

3. You are not being talked about online. This is erroneous thinking. It is highly probable that someone has talked about you online or is talking about you online be it through chatting with a friend via Facebook, or posting a feedback on review or local business listing site. Contrary to this assumption, potential customers can easily unearth such information simply by conducting a search for you. The reality is that if they discover negative information they are more likely than not to go to your competitor who has a clean record.

4. It is okay to ignore the harmful things posted online as they will disappear of their own accord after sometime. This is wrong. Ignoring the negative online contents will not make them go away. Anything and everything has the potential of going viral online and no one can determine what does. This is why it is important to handle any negative online content immediately and appropriately before it goes out of hand. Sometimes all it takes is one negative comment to wipe out years of having a good reputation and it takes time to repair the damage once it has been done. It is therefore better to safeguard your reputation by constantly keeping it

monitored so that the necessary steps can be taken to keep the reputation in good stance.

5. Negative contents posted online can be easily deleted. This is untrue. Content posted online tend to stay on permanently and are almost impossible to remove sometimes. One of the policies of a number of review websites is that content posted will not be removed. In some other instances where content can be deleted, they can still be reposted and reshared, there are no guarantees that they will not reappear again elsewhere.

6. It is not necessary to think about taking steps to manage you online reputation until you are faced with issues regarding your reputation. This is a severe blunder. Prevention is always better than cure, it is so much easier to maintain a good reputation than to try and repair a damaged one. In actual fact it is less complicated to establish a reputation from a non-existent online presence than it is to salvage a damaged reputation. Online reputation management encompasses diligently monitoring what is being said about you and responding appropriately. In addition to that, it also entails creating positive content about you and posting them strategically online. The advantage of doing this is that if adverse content is posted online there will be more than sufficient positive materials online to cushion the effect. It is imperative to build a robust, positive reputation for your company to avoid the hassle of trying to salvage a ruined reputation in the future.

7. Online reputation management is strictly needed and used by big organisations. This is a fallacy. Every person or organisation should have their online reputation managed because any organisation or person's reputation can be

ruined at any point in time. No person or organisation has immunity against such attacks.

8. For as long as content is shared privately then it is safe. This is false. You could have been savvy enough to set your privacy settings; however the people you are sharing your content with may be resharing and reposting your content without you being aware of this. In essence what this means is that even content that you deem private can get public exposure, the lesson here is to exercise caution when posting content online. In some instances it is content that other people have shared about you that can tarnish reputation, hence for monitoring reputation.

9. People or companies that have bad reputations must have done something to surely deserve them. This is not correct. The crux of the matter is that every person and organisation is vulnerable and can be targeted. It could be by irate exes, disgruntled ex-employees, nasty competitors, or even strangers can attack a person or company for no apparent reason or to get back at them.

10. You can control what is being said about you online. That is impossible. It is not conceivable to control what others post about you or your business online. There is no saying what they choose to post; it could be positive or negative. Nevertheless, the fact that you are not able to what they are saying does not justify not being proactive and doing something about it.

11. Search Engine Optimisation (SEO) is not essential for managing reputation. This is incorrect. SEO is vitally needed to help control the sort of information that will be displayed about you on the first page of the search engines

and Google in particular. Employing SEO strategies will help drive positive content high up in the search engines while pushing down any negative content to the bottom of the search results. There is a risk of negative remarks and posts about your company showing up high in the search results without using SEO to determine the outcome of search results.

12. Negative online reputation can be easily covered up. This absolutely not true, it cannot be done. As soon as negative posts have been broadcasted online, it is out there in public. It cannot be retrieved and it cannot be concealed. Actually attempting to cover up merely causes the negative posts to blow up and attract more unwanted attention.

Challenges of Online Reputation Management

Successful online reputation management is feasible however; there are a number of challenges that one would have to overcome in order to achieve this.

1. Everything posted online whether positive or negative tends to remain indefinitely, so invariably if a reputation is damaged online those damaging posts will almost certainly never go away. Moreover, most sites where people can post negative reviews have policies stating that original complaints irrespective of its truth or validity will not be removed.

2. The "world wide web" is not unlegislated, however the legal landscape is ambiguous and the lines are blurred, they are not clear cut in many instances. Though, the prescribed legal structure is progressively altering to meet the specific challenges posed by the digital revolution. Established laws are being adapted and applied in unique ways to exploit the online environment and gain competitive advantage. Incorporate legal strategy into your crisis prevention and response plans to reduce your chance of ending up as a very public test case.

3. In spite of exercising great care your social media platform could be hijacked by activists or even customers to further their own agenda and lend a voice to their grievances or protests.

4. Social media somehow has an inclination to magnify negative expressions over positive ones, it is imperative therefore to strike the right balance and know when to

respond in public, when not to and when to take discussions offline. This is a critical scale that needs to be weighed with the utmost care and concern in order to elude a notorious 'social media devastation'.

5. Managing your reputation is crucial but more important than that, is really what your company stands for. No matter how hard you work at protecting your reputation if your company behaves unethically or its products or services are inferior in quality then it will be hard to safeguard your reputation as people will talk about their bad experiences online and ruin your reputation. Your reputation can only reflect what you stand for. Like Abraham Lincoln said "Character is like a tree and reputation like its shadow. The shadow is what we think of it; the tree is the real thing."

6. Human beings have two ears and one mouth so that they can listen twice as much as they can speak. This is a big challenge with managing reputation as the propensity is to respond generally more than listening, meanwhile the key skill to develop is to listen twice as much as responding. Don't just immediately react and respond to social media posts without taking the necessary action of listening attentively to the messages behind the negative posts or reviews. Pay keen attention to what is been said and deal with the root of any issues that you have, otherwise history will keep repeating itself. See such times as opportunities to take an inventory, make appropriate corrections and weed out lurking issues that caused the initial dilemma where applicable.

7. Online reputation management is still very much in the elementary stages and so the procedures and practices governing it are evolving and therefore subject to change.

8. Everyone can speak and be heard in social media, this has immense advantages but also enormous disadvantages in that a disgruntled ex-employee of customer or even competitor can vent their ill-feelings towards you and say what they like regardless of its truth and that voice will be heard in the digital world. No one verifies the validity of what is being said before it is published to the whole world online. The effect is that reputation can be easily tarnished by one voice online.

9. It is relatively easy for people with similar negative comments about certain issues to link up on the internet because of online social and web search. This just enables the little spark started by one person to gather momentum and get bigger to the detriment of the company.

10. Companies need to have skilful people who can not only monitor online reputation but also be able to comprehend the data collated from their monitoring perations. They also need to know the successive tactics that must be implemented.

11. Investing the time to get social online and being proactive about finding out where the loyal customers are and then building an online community of contented customers who are happy to leave wonderful comments and positive feedback.

12. Putting an end to having their heads stuck in the sand, ignoring or underestimating the power and influence of social media. Understanding that having no social media presence at all can sometime be just as detrimental as having a negative online reputation. If you have no online presence then you leave your disgruntled customers no choice but to leave their comments on Facebook, Yelp or other similar social media platforms, therefore leaving your reputation in their hands!

13. Knowing how to respond to complaints from customers and taking the right steps to curtail issues. It is vital not to have a myopic view when considering the expense involved in making a disgruntled customer happy. The lifetime value of the customer that could potentially be lost and the damage one customer can do to the company's reputation should always be given serious consideration. Many a companies have overlooked this and paid dearly in the long run.

14. Making the right choice of either eating humble pie or saying sorry which is your best and safest option or digging your heels in and remaining stubborn which is the more expensive route to take.

15. Bad news travels mega fast online. It is incredible how negative, dramatic broadcast spreads rapidly and gain so much visibility within hours online on social media platforms such as Facebook, YouTube, Twitter and eventually on search engines. All it takes is for the item to go viral online and in a matter of hours, millions of people would have seen it and the news item could have traveled around a number of countries.

16. It is very challenging to outline the demographics of the audience that would be reached by the internet publicity. This makes it hard to gauge the extent of the damage sometimes.

17. Online reputation management is complicated, assuming an excessively stringent approach or the incorrect part in efforts to control social media crisis may end up causing more woes.

18. It can sometimes be almost impossible to identify the person who posted online anonymously or by using a pseudo name. In theory, an application to the ourt can be made to compel an ISP or platform supplier to divulge an internet publisher's identity.

19. Furthermore there are a host of legal ramifications that needs to be considered in some cases. The question of jurisdiction comes in to play a great deal in the "world wide web" as what is illegal in one country could be legal in another so the question is - the rule of law of which country will take precedence in cases where two or more different countries are involved? For instance Person A lives in the U.K buys a product from Person B who lives in France and leaves a negative review on Person C's site (Person C lives in the U.S.A).The rule of law of which land would the issues be considered under?

20. The time factor involved in the issues of online reputation. It takes a short span of time for a reputation to get damaged as news travel so fast online and can travel worldwide in a matter of hours. However, in the same vein restoring damaged reputation takes a lot of time, there are no quick fixes.

21. Reputation can be damaged on the basis of something that is totally false, this seems completely unjustified. A disgruntled ex-employee, competitor or even a nasty customer can easily bring a reputation down simply by posting something negative, this really gives too much power to an individual. There seems to be no way to defend or fight for the reputation. The system seems completely unfair as the consumers can criticise the accused, without having to face them and the accused seemingly has no right of defence.

22. Educating employees on social media strategies and having a strategic plan for handling possible issues both internal and external issues is imperative.

Your Company's Online Reputation

Your online image is NOT just your business website. There is much more to it. Google says this:
"Your online identity is determined not only by what you post, but also by what others post about you — whether a mention in a blog post, a photo tag or a reply to a public status update,"
- Google

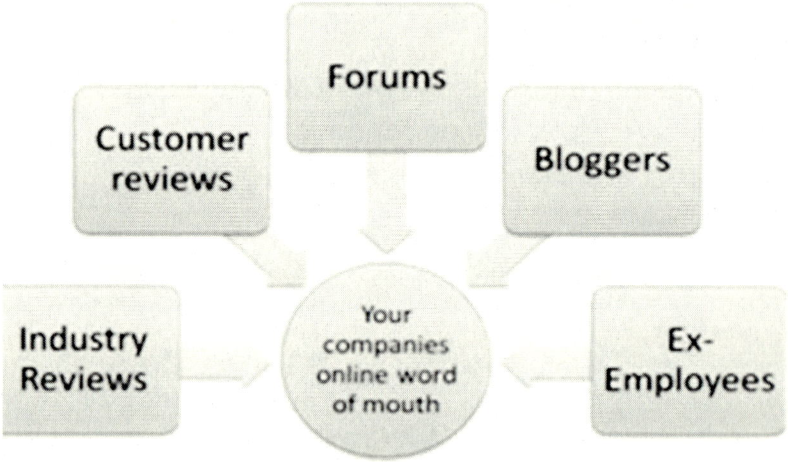

In a nutshell, your online reputation consists of everything about your business that exists online. The array of materials that could potentially influence your company's online reputation is wider than you might realise at first.

Here are just some components of your online image:

1. Remarks made about your business on social media such as Twitter or Facebook.
2. Pictures about your company that can be found online.
3. Videos about your business whether good or bad on Vimeo, YouTube and other video sharing sites.

4. Posts and articles published on blogs and elsewhere online about your business.
5. Geo-location information broadcast through services like Foursquare, Gowalla, Brightkite etc.
6. Comments that others make about you in social media or in blog posts.

7. Images of your business that others publish on social media.

Even what people say in an email or through instant messaging could potentially be copied and made public.

In fact, if you're beginning to feel like virtually anything that others do on the internet could become part of your business' online reputation, then you're starting to get the picture.

Now throw in the mobile internet and smart phones, where people can read and write reviews from anywhere. You can see how a bad review about your business will hit harder and spread faster than ever before.

What is being said about your business?

Potential customers will frequently look at all results provided by search engines not only your website, but review sites, discussion forums, etc. When they browse down the list, what are the things that stand out about your company? Are they all positive, appropriate, current information? Are there any harmful listings stating negative things about your company? If the information people come across during a search relating to your company is adverse, it can affect the decisions they make. Negative information can ultimately lead to problems in many areas including sales, investor relations, recruitment, financials, image and reputation. In other words – it can inflict damage to your brand.

Are you aware of what is being said about you online? If you do not know you are treading on dangerous grounds. It is imperative to have an ear to the ground by monitoring what is being said about you on a constant basis. This will help you maintain your reputation online and also help you protect it against any potential threats.

The first step you can take to finding out what people are saying about your business online is to merely Google your company name.

The questions to ask are as follows:

Are there any reviews about your company on the first page? If there are, are they good or bad? An example of reviews on Google can be seen below:

1. How many spots do your business own on the first page? The more positive spots you have on the first page of Google the better. Look at these results for Rainbow Pharmacy:

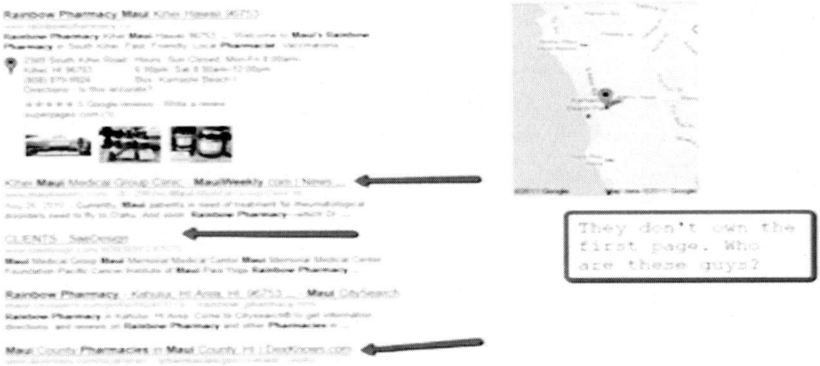

Do you have positive content and reviews past the first page? If so, moving these items to the first page of Google would help your online reputation.

Getting Google Love for Your Small Business

To get your positive content to the first page of Google, focus on search engine optimization (SEO) for these items. Good SEO strategies, by default, combat negative mentions. SEO typically takes at least three months before your business will see an impact, but the long-term value is unlike any other online marketing effort.

Your goal is to own the first page of Google for your business name with all positive content. Remember, 95% of all searchers will never go past the first page.

If you look at the search results below, you will see that Grand Wailea has positive content all over the first and second pages.

What if there are negative reviews and comments on the first page?

Be careful. How you respond to these negative items is critical to your business.

The biggest thing you can be proactive about when it comes to your business' online reputation is to actively seek reviews. The two biggest are Google and Yelp.

You might not know that Google has an online business directory called Google Places. These listings are free and compiled by Google from various online directories like the online Yellow Pages.

Here is what a place page looks like:

Here is how a place page shows up in Google search results:

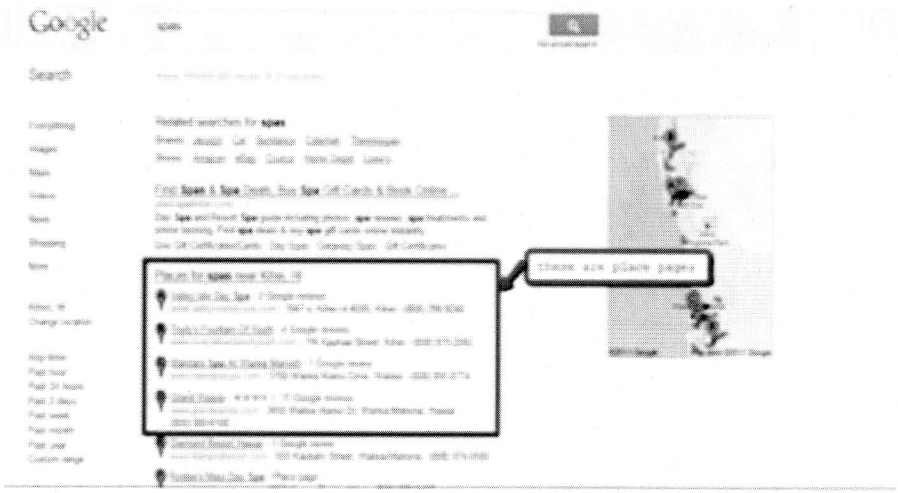

Why Online Reputation Matters To CEOS/Top Executives

A CEOs reputation is a vital aspect of a company's reputation. The truth is that people evaluate and judge a business by the reputation of its CEO/ Top Executives. This means that potential customers search for the name of the CEO/ Top Executives online to read what they can find out about them when deciding where to do business. It is therefore imperative that thought provoking measures are taking on safeguarding both your personal brand and reputation.

An organisation with CEOs/ Top Executives that has negative perceptions online invariably contaminates the organisation or the brand. This is in terms of online postings, social mentions in blogs, microblogs, and/or news results that about that person.

Research states that 87% of people think that a CEO's reputation mirrors the company's reputation generally. In other words, there is an inclination that media for the company as a whole is negative when the CEOs have bad reputation.
Reputation is evidently a high risk factor for CEOs and their organisations. CEOs must therefore work hard to create and uphold a positive reputation for their own sakes as well as for their companies.

Classic examples can be seen below:-

Case Study 1

This story was taken from The Daily Mail [1]

In February 2011, Kenneth Cole posted a tweet where he used the enormously grim events in Cairo to promote his brand. The background of the story is that there was a riot in Cairo, at least 24 people were killed and over 200 injured in Cairo during a protest that broke out because of an attack on a church.

The original tweet can be seen below:-

The tweet was signed "-KC" indicating that the error had the Kenneth Cole's consent before going public.

People who read the tweet were livid and upset. A number of people reacted with negative remarks that Kenneth Cole would take what was going on in Egypt so flippantly, or compare his brand and the dire situation in Egypt.

Some of the responses are as follows:

'Keep it classy @KennethCole. Never shopping there again. . . ,' wrote one.

Another said: 'You should be ashamed of yourselves @KennethCole ! How tasteless and insensitive! People are dying there!'

Kenneth Cole apologised within one hour of the post and the original tweet was later deleted".

The apology stated as follows:- " we weren't intending to make light of a serious situation. We understand the sensitivity of this historic moment." The tweet was initialed "KC" [2] this gave an indication that Cole wrote it. The apology further stated "I apologize to everyone who was offended by my insensitive tweet about the situation in Egypt," Kenneth Cole also made the following comment on his official Facebook account. "I've dedicated my life to raising awareness about serious social issues, and in hindsight my attempt at humor regarding a nation liberating themselves against oppression was poorly timed and absolutely inappropriate." [2]

Kenneth Cole's decision to apologise promptly was right and he should be commended for that. The apology would have gone a long way to repair the potential damage that could have ensued.

Case Study 2

This was extracted from NY Post [3]

On the 10th June 2015, Alejandro Rhett, the vice president of J.Crew's men's merchandising department had the unenviable of task of personally telling 175 employees that they were being laid off.

Regrettably, pictures surfaced a few hours after on Instagram showing him and a colleague partying at a New York City bar close to the company's headquarters. The photo was hash tagged "The Hunger Games."

Alejandro Rhett even compared himself to one of the characters in "Mean Girls," a classic teen movie, saying, "On Wednesdays we wear monochrome pleated shorts."

He also used the tag #nofunhere for a group selfie taken by Andrew Ruth - J.Crew's retail men's merchandiser.

All the pictures were deleted. An insider from J.Crew condemned both the timing and Rhett's "poor judgment."
"It's just inappropriate that you'd be out drinking when people on your team had been laid off," and further stated that "J.Crew has serious issues right now, and no one in the office had a smile on their face that day."
A spokesperson from J.Crew spokesman said that the company "does not condone" the behavior of Rhett and the others, adding, "As soon as we were made aware, the appropriate actions took place."

Case Study 3

This was culled from The Daily Mail [4]

Rakesh "Rocky" Agrawal the Director of global strategy was fired in May 2014 by Paypal after he used Twitter as a means of hauling insults at some colleagues including Christina Smedley - PayPal's vice president of global communications.

One tweet said:-

"Duck you Smedley you useless middle. Manager"

He also tweeted –

"Christina Smedley is a useless. Piece of s**t."

The tweets were subsequently deleted. However, Paypal were quick to take action and they tweeted the following:-

"Rakesh Agrawal is no longer with the company. Treat everyone with respect. No excuses. PayPal has zero tolerance."

The tweet can be seen below:-

PayPal
@PayPal
Follow

Rakesh Agrawal is no longer with the company. Treat everyone with respect. No excuses. PayPal has zero tolerance.

10:16 PM - 3 May 2014

312 RETWEETS 257 FAVORITES

Case Study 4

This was extracted from The Huffington Post [5]

In December 2013, Greg Gopman, the CEO of AngelHack purportedly posted the following provocative statement on Facebook:-

“Just got back to SF. I’ve traveled around the world and I gotta say there is nothing more grotesque than walking down market st in San Francisco,” he further wrote. ”Why the heart of our city has to be overrun by crazy, homeless, drug dealers, dropouts, and trash I have no clue. Each time I pass it my love affair with SF dies a little.”

Gopman complained further about the behaviour of such “degenerates” saying:-
“The difference is in other cosmopolitan cities, the lower part of society keep to themselves. They sell small trinkets, beg coyly, stay quiet, and generally stay out of your way. They realize it’s a privilege to be in the civilized part of town and view themselves as guests,”

“In downtown SF the degenerates gather like hyenas, spit, urinate, taunt you, sell drugs, get rowdy, they act like they own the center of the city... It a disgrace... You can preach compassion, equality, and be the biggest lover in the world, but there is an area of town for degenerates and an area of town for the working class.”

This post was later removed amidst a torrid of criticisms on social media networks, some of them can seen below:-.

Matt May
@mattmay

Follow

I can think of one way Angelhack CEO Greg Gopman could help solve SF's "human trash" problem. Move. (Not to Seattle.) valleywag.gawker.com/happy-holidays...

4:33 PM - 11 Dec 2013

Happy Holidays: Startup CEO Complains SF Is Full of Human...
Behold a perfect Silicon Valley denizen, an archetype: he's been written up in TechCrunch for his hackathon-organizing company.
valleywag.gawker.com

4 3

Another tweet below:

Christopher
@christophernies

Follow

I will never participate in another @Angelhack event. @Gopmania, this is absolutely vile. facebook.com/Gopman/posts/1...

3:29 PM - 11 Dec 2013

2

The next day, Gopman uploaded another post onto Facebook, apologising for his comments:-

Last night, I made inappropriate comments about San Francisco and its less fortunate citizens on Market st. I'm really sorry for my comments. I trivialized the plight of those struggling to get by and I shouldn't have. I hope this thread can help start an open discussion on what changes we can make to fix these serious problems. Again, I am deeply sorry.

However, it seemed like he had done some damage already as some more posts criticising him were still posted after the apology.

Michael Endler
@InfoMEndler
Follow

I know he apologized, but @AngelHack CEO's comments are a perfect microcosm for SF's new rich and its view on income inequaility #shameful
6:31 PM - 11 Dec 2013

4 5

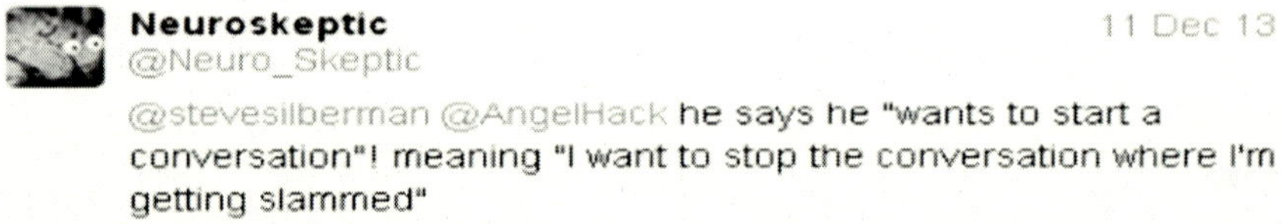

Neuroskeptic
@Neuro_Skeptic
11 Dec 13

@stevesilberman @AngelHack he says he "wants to start a conversation"! meaning "I want to stop the conversation where I'm getting slammed"

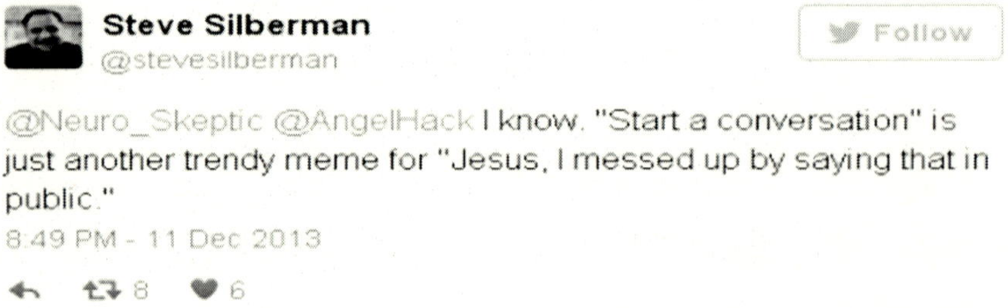

Steve Silberman
@stevesilberman
Follow

@Neuro_Skeptic @AngelHack I know. "Start a conversation" is just another trendy meme for "Jesus, I messed up by saying that in public."
8:49 PM - 11 Dec 2013

8 6

Sabeen Ali, the founder of Angel Hack distanced the organisation from Gopman's post and stated that Gopman had stepped down and was no longer with them. The content of the post can be read below [6]:-

Dear Community,
"I know a lot of you have read the articles in response to Greg's Facebook post regarding the homeless issue in San Francisco. I'd like to first respond by saying that those opinions do not reflect those of AngelHack or the opinions of any other AngelHack employee."

"Furthermore, Greg stepped down as CEO of AngelHack in October 2013 to pursue other business ventures. A formal announcement of his resignation was planned for this month following the finale of our 2013 hackathon series. However, in light of recent events, we have decided to disclose early that there has been a change and that Greg is no longer CEO nor has he taken an active role in the company since October."

"AngelHack is an organization comprised of compassionate employees and Ambassadors from all around the world. Our collective mission as an organization is to empower developers and the entrepreneurial community. Most of our employees, including myself, have taken part in many non-profit initiatives that serve underprivileged communities and we are committed to doing so in the future."

Case Study 5

This story was from the Huffington Post [7]

In August 2013, Peter Shih, the founder of Celery - payment start-up company posted what was supposed to be a satire on his blog titled “10 Things I Hate About You: San Francisco Edition.” He was basically bad mouthing San Francisco, the city he was now living in.

The outcry on Twitter happened within hours, there was even a blog post by BuzzFeed titled “10 Things I Hate About Peter Shih.” [8]

Shih amended the post and posted a disclaimer:

“Disclaimer: This post is an opinion piece by me. It was intended to be humorous satire. Hate all you want, but please stop bringing my company into this.”

This obviously did not placate the people of San Francisco. Posters were put up on the streets calling for a boycotting of Shih’s company and advising him to move back to New York.

See photo below:-

On the 17th August, 2013 PCMag published a post regarding Shih's apology [9]:-

"I want to sincerely apologize to everyone who read my poorly written blog post about San Francisco. I made idiotic and childish, but worse yet, thoughtless, hurtful and offensive comments that I am deeply sorry about," wrote Shih in a blog post, published today. "There are no excuses for my poor judgment, so I make none. I take full responsibility that this mistake was completely my own."

"I don't deserve any forgiveness for the stupidity of my actions and words, but I sincerely hope to demonstrate by my future behavior to humbly build up and not tear down the communities and people around me," he added.

Key lessons:

It is important to bear in mind that as a CEO or Senior Executive of a company what you post on Social Media platforms does not just affect you personally, it has a major impact on the company as well. It is therefore imperative that you exercise due caution on Social Media platforms.

Mistakes sometimes happen, the vital thing is to promptly take corrective actions to rectify the situation.

References

[1] http://www.dailymail.co.uk/news/article-1353376/Egypt-twitter-Kenneth-Cole-sparks-outrage-bad-taste-tweet-Cairo-riots.html

[2] http://money.cnn.com/2011/02/03/news/companies/KennethCole_twitter/

[3] http://nypost.com/2015/06/17/j-crew-exec-brags-about-surviving-hunger-games-layoffs/

[4] http://www.dailymail.co.uk/news/article-2620526/No-excuses-zero-tolerance-PayPal-exec-FIRED-bizarre-late-night-Twitter-rant-against-colleagues.html#ixzz48GOM0d8W

[5] http://www.huffingtonpost.com/2013/12/11/angelhack-san-francisco_n_4428104.html

[6] http://angelhack.com/2013/12/03/in-response-to-gregory-gopmans-facebook-post/

[7] http://www.huffingtonpost.com/2013/08/16/peter-shih_n_3768505.html

[8] https://www.buzzfeed.com/typo/10-things-i-hate-about-peter-shih-9lu0

[9] http://uk.pcmag.com/web-sites-products/13517/news/startup-co-founder-peter-shih-apologizes-for-san-francisco-r

Why Online Reputation Matters For Non-Profits/Public Sector Organisations

Non-profit establishments are even more reliant on their reputation than companies as a non-profit organisation will cease to exist if it loses the backing of its donors.
People tend to donate to Non-profit organisations mainly when they are convinced that they are reputable organisations with worthy causes.

More so, a Non-profit needs to protect its reputation as it can be prohibited from serving the community which is their main reason for existing in the first place if it has an adverse reputation.

Case Study 1

Story is from the Huffington Post [1]

The Red Cross had to intervene to avert an incident that potentially could have threatened its reputation.

In February 2011, a social media specialist for the American Red Cross accidentally tweeted something that was meant for a personal account on the institution's account.

The tweet can be seen below:

The Red Cross promptly responded by apologising and making the situation light-hearted, they also guaranteed their followers that "the Red Cross [was] sober":

The Red Cross were able to turn the situation around to their advantage; they added more followers, got more donations and a lot of good press.

Case Study 2

Story is from The Independent [2]

Transport for London (TFL) committed a social media blunder on the 3rd April, 2014 with their response on Twitter to a dissatisfied customer.

Twitter user @dan_down had tweeted, “Sort it out @LDNOverground. If I’m late once more this month I lose 25 per cent of my salary. Are you lot reimbursing me?”
Tweet can be seen below:-

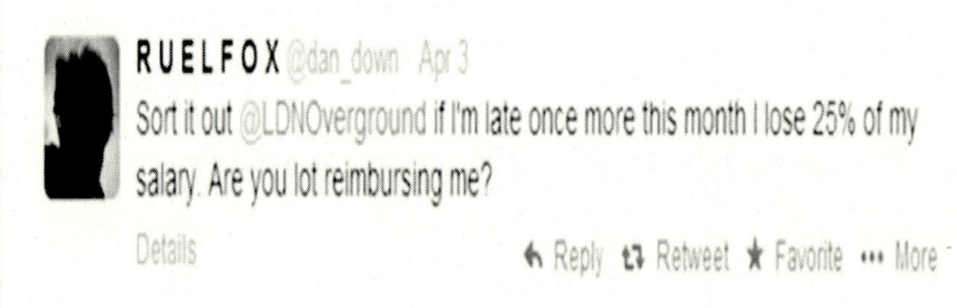

TFL had obviously not thought through their response and so decided to give their customer some sensible, practical advice, tweeting back: - “@dan_down Leave early you will not be late next time. Hope this helps.”

Tweet can be seen below:-

@dan_down condemned TFL's "smart arse answers" and that TFL should "stick to your timetable". He told them that he expects their services would be on time when he gets to the station. He went on to say - "How dare you answer like that," "Why should I have to compensate for your shoddy service.

Why not run on time?"

TFL eventually backed down and tweeted "Apologies for the response you received earlier. I don't think it was meant to come across like that. I'll get this looked into."

Unfortunately, @dan-down did not accept the apology tweeting back – "I'm afraid I'm not accepting apologies this time. I've emailed customer services in the hope that it's taken seriously." "This can't be brushed aside with an insincere 'sorry'."

A number of Twitter users were also quick to jump in and criticise TFL for their response as well:-

@carole136 tweeted: "OMG is this a serious response to a customer? How arrogant of you!!!"

@carolinehonour said: "How much time exactly should we be expected to leave early by? 3 hours? 5? Really quite surprised by your glibness."

Case Study 3

Story is from The Guardian [3]

Croydon council had to shut down its Twitter account after someone mistakenly posted a remark criticising the abilities of an Evening Standard journalist, saying “a squirrel could have run rings” around them. The writer’s original intention was to send a private message. However, in frustration, sent a public tweet and aired their personal thoughts publicly through the account of the council and therefore on the council’s behalf. This was extremely embarrassing for the council and it portrayed them in an unprofessional light.

Case Study 4

Story is from The Daily Post [4]

In May 2014 Wrexham Council accidentally called its own executive board “pathetic” whilst posting live updates on Twitter. @wrexhamcbc tweet read: “Pathetic Exec Board agree the recommendations, including a deferral on the grounds maintenance budget for 15/16.”

Tweet can be seen below:-

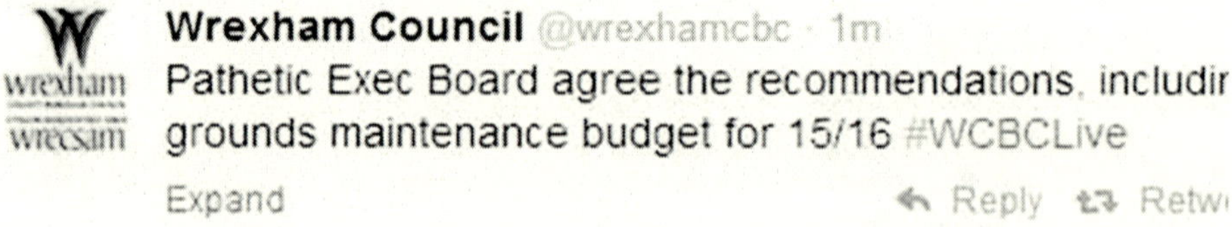

Some eagle eyed Twitter users spotted the error and were quick to point it out.

The response was: "Oops! Proof why men are no good at multi-tasking."

Another tweet read: "I'll get it right this time...Exec Board agree the recommendations, including a deferral on the grounds maintenance budget for 15/16 #WCBC."

However a Twitter user from the account @AledRobertsAM tweeted as follows: "Personally I welcome the council's new found transparency in describing its own Executive Board as pathetic."

A spokesman from Wrexham Council stated: "We hold our hands (and big sausage fingers) up - we fell victim to the dreaded predictive text. We noticed our error and the tweet was removed promptly."

Case Study 5

Story is from MSNBC [5]

In April 2014, The New York City Police Department encouraged New Yorkers to tweet photos of themselves with police officers and use the hashtag #myNYPD.

They said they may feature such photos on their Facebook page.

However, this social media interaction venture went awry very quickly. The NYPD obviously were not expecting the responses they got as people uploaded images of police violence on Twitter.

A few of the photos, some quite disturbing can be seen below:-

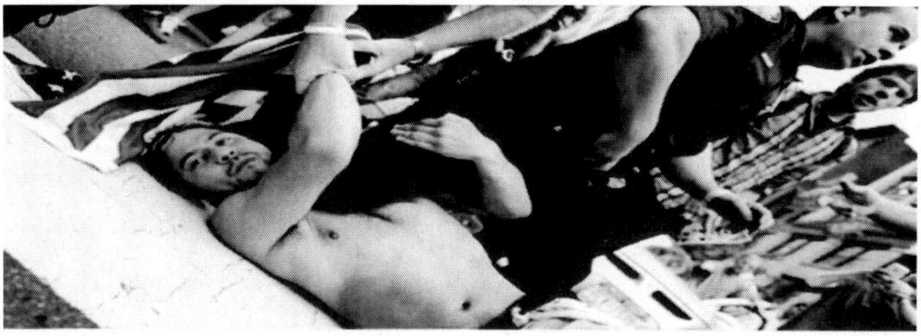

Bardock Obama
@TheBardockObama

Follow

You might not have known this, but the NYPD can help you with that kink in your neck. #myNYPD
9:32 PM - 23 Apr 2014

504 466

DefendedInTheStreets
@KimaniFilm

Follow

how #myNYPD treats 16 year olds who say "no" to being stopped and frisked: youtube.com/watch?v=BlwdlO...
8:42 PM - 22 Apr 2014

216 · 75

Cocky McSwagsalot
@MoreAndAgain

Follow

If you can't walk, don't worry, the NYPD will carry you. How helpful!
#myNYPD
9:20 PM - 22 Apr 2014

241 67

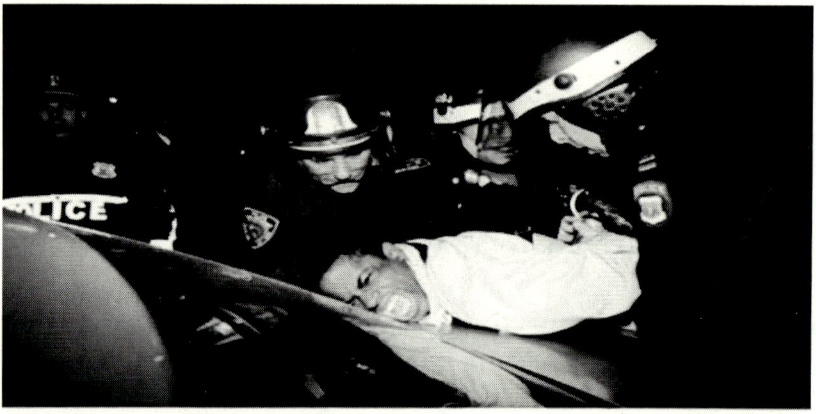

Occupy Wall Street
@OccupyWallStNYC

Follow

Free Massages from the #NYPD. What does YOUR Police Department offer? Tweet at #MyNYPD
8:13 PM - 22 Apr 2014

678 272

Casey Aldridge
@CaseyJAldridge

Follow

"And we're going to have to run you over, just for good measure." #myNYPD

9:30 PM - 22 Apr 2014

601 221

immigrant
@shushugah

Follow

#NYPD Keeping the Streets Safe. Show some love, and send your pics with #MyNYPD hashtags!

8:16 PM - 22 Apr 2014

139 66

Occupy Wall Street
@OccupyWallStNYC

Follow

Here the #NYPD engages with its community members, changing hearts and minds one baton at a time. #myNYPD

8:12 PM - 22 Apr 2014

1,434 564

Case Study 6

Story is from The Guardian

On the 24th of August 2014, the British embassy in Washington tweeted a picture that was meant to be light-hearted to celebrate the 200th anniversary of when the British troops burnt the White House.

The picture was one of a cake with a model of the White House placed on it as well as both the British and American flags, which were surrounded by lighted fireworks.

The following was tweeted alongside the picture: "Commemorating the 200th anniversary of burning the White House. Only sparklers this time!"

Picture can be seen below:-

The British embassy's tweet was retweeted more than 4,000 times.

A number of Twitter users understandably did not see the humour at all. Someone named Yossi Gestetner asked: “WWHHAATT??? Is this suppose to be funny?”

Another tweeted: "I think this is in extremely POOR TASTE."

An apology was issued on the account two hours after the original message, saying:-

"Apologies for earlier Tweet." Adding: "We meant to mark an event in history & celebrate our strong friendship today."

Lessons to be learnt from this are as follows:

Employees can never be too careful when posting on social media, so exercise caution so you can avoid mistakes of posting on corporate social media platforms instead of personal ones.

Take responsibility for mistakes and apologise for them. Be transparent, do not try to cover up anything, the public can be forgiving on social media when they see that you have been straight with them.

Using humour, if done in the right manner can curb potential social media disasters. It must be done discriminatingly though.

References

[1] http://www.huffingtonpost.com/2011/02/16/red-cross-rogue-tweet_n_824114.html

[2] http://www.independent.co.uk/news/uk/home-news/annoyed-commuter-in-twitter-spat-with-transport-for-london-9237895.html

[3] http://www.theguardian.com/public-leaders-network/2014/nov/28/public-sector-social-media-blunders

[4] http://www.dailypost.co.uk/news/north-wales-news/wrexham-council-describes-executive-board-7114945

[5] http://www.msnbc.com/the-last-word/nypd-misfires-its-twitter-campaign

[6] http://www.theguardian.com/world/2014/aug/25/british-embassy-tweet-white-house-burning-1814

Why Online Reputation Matters to Businesses

There are a number of reasons why having a good reputation is important to individuals and organisations alike.

The main difference between a business's online reputation and its offline reputation is the fact that the online reputation is easily accessible to everyone so it is harder to hide. It is imperative that every business manages its online reputation no matter what type of business it is big or small, online or offline.

Case Study 1

Story is from The Daily Mail [1]

In November 2013, Home Depot Inc., the giant Home improvement firm issued an apology for a racist tweet that was posted as part of a promotional campaign they were running.

The tweet in question revealed a photo of two African-American drummers and another drummer in the middle wearing a gorilla mask, with a question: “Which drummer is not like the others?”

The tweet was swiftly deleted, but unfortunately, some people had already taken screen shots of it and this was disseminated far and wide on social media. The tweet was also a news item on both NBC and CNBC, amongst others.

Home Depot apologised profusely tweeting numerous times:-

The Home Depot
@HomeDepot

Which drummer is not like the others? See more @CollegeGameDay pics at hdgameday.com #HDgameday #football

Home Depot further went on to say that they had dismissed both the person and outside agency that was guilty of posting the tweet.

Stephen Holmes, spokesman for the Atlanta-based company said “We have zero tolerance for anything so stupid and offensive,” He went on to add that the company is 'closely' revising their social media measures to ascertain “how this could have happened, and how to ensure it never happens again.”

Case Study 2

Story is from CNET [2]

In September, 2014 LG made an attempt to mock Apple's #bendgate by tweeting from their France account saying "Our smartphones don't bend, they are naturally curved ;)."

The tweet that was sent is below, obviously in French:-

The tweet could possibly have scored them a few points, but unfortunately it backfired as it had been sent from an iPhone. The joke ended up being on LG, it was clearly embarrassing.

Case Study 3

Story is from CNN [3]

Whilst the country was coming to grips with the shooting incident that happened in Colorado where 12 people were killed, the National Rifle Association tweeted the following:- "Good morning, shooters. Happy Friday! Weekend plans?"

That tweet went out at 9:20 a.m. shortly after the shooting; it was deleted at about 12:30 p.m.

Twitter users swiftly condemned the tweet because of the timing.

A Twitter user @ambermac tweeted:- "Perhaps NRA should read news before tweeting."

Andrew Arulanandam NRA spokesman made the following comment to CNN "A single individual, unaware of events in Colorado, tweeted a comment that is being completely taken out of context."

He went on to say: "Our thoughts and prayers are with the victims, their families and the community. NRA will not have any further comment until all the facts are known."

Case Study 4

Story is from Sky News [4]

In March 2013, Luton Airport put up a seemingly light-hearted post on their Facebook Page to reassure their customers about safety despite any snow falls.

The post stated: “Because we are such a super airport....this is what we prevent you from when it snows......Weeeee :)” and a photo of a plane crash was added, unfortunately it was the picture of a real-life plane crash that happened at Chicago Midway Airport in 2005. A six-year old car passenger was killed when the plane collided with his family car.

The photo was deleted about 75 minutes after being posted, however enraged Facebook users vented their anger at Luton Airport.

Luton airport "apologised unreservedly" for the post and called it "wholly unacceptable and insensitive". It stated: "We have Social Media guidelines in place which clearly set out what is acceptable, however in this instance a new member of our external social media agency made a misguided mistake which resulted in a breach of those guidelines.

"The post was put up at 09:15 yesterday morning and was removed shortly after 10:30. Two individuals have been suspended from the account."

<u>Case Study 5</u>

Story is from The Telegraph [5]

In January 2013, Tesco sent out an automated tweet to more than 47,000 followers saying "it's sleepy time so we're off to hit the hay! See you at 8am for more #TescoTweets"

On a good day, this would have been fine and completely harmless, however on this occasion the tweet happened to have gone out in the middle of a PR crisis about horsemeat which had allegedly been found in Tesco's frozen meals.

A Tesco official tweeted an apology saying "I'm terribly sorry. That tweet was scheduled before we knew of the current situation. We'd never intend to make light of it."

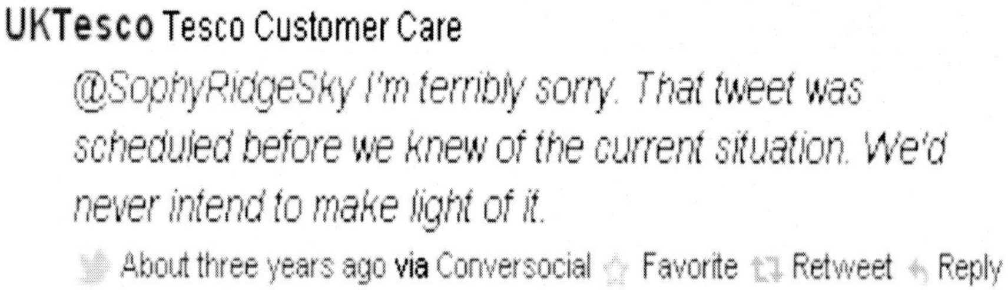

Case Study 6

Story is from The Daily Mail [6]

In September 2013, after British Airways lost Hassan Syed's father's luggage, he decided to make his complaint on Twitter by paying for Promoted Tweets to show his dissatisfaction about how British Airways were handling the situation.

Advertisers tend to purchase promoted tweets when they want to broaden their audience reach, the promoted tweets are displayed prominently in the Twitter feed of their targeted viewers. The promoted tweets also show up in search results for a trend that is being promoted and in some instances on the timelines of users'. At the same time promoted tweets can be retweeted by anyone so is similar to normal tweets.

Mr Syed's promoted tweet targeted the UK and New York markets but it obviously did not advertise British Airways favourably.
Mr Syed's promoted tweet said: “Don't fly @BritishAirways. Their customer service is horrendous.”

See screen shot of tweet below:-

British Airways however, did not respond to this tweet until after four hours. Unfortunately because of the time lapse, the tweet had already been seen by 25000 Twitter users within six hours.

British Airways responded to Mr Syed through a direct message after four hours saying: “Sorry for the delay in responding, our twitter feed is open 09:00-17:00 GMT. Please DM [direct message] your baggage ref and we'll look into this.”

British Airways later apologised for the incident saying: “We would like to apologise to the customer for the inconvenience caused. We have been in contact with the customer and the bag is due to be delivered today.”

Case Study 7

Story is from The Guardian [7]

In January 2013, HMV (a UK entertainment retailer) found themselves in trouble and so laid off a number of staff which obviously did not sit well with a number of them. One of the laid off members of staff still had access to the Company's official Twitter account - @hmvtweets and seized the opportunity to post live tweets of about what was going on in the company.

The first tweet broadcasted: "We're tweeting live from HR where we're all being fired! Exciting!!!"

The next one read : "There are over 60 of us being fired at once! Mass execution, of loyal employees who love the brand. #hmvXFactorFiring,"

Another tweet said: "Sorry we've been quiet for so long," ... "Under contract, we've been unable to say a word, or – more importantly – tell the truth."

The disgruntled laid off employees also briefly explained the reason for their protest on Twitter stating: "Under usual circumstances, we'd never dare do such a thing as this," they stated. "However, when the company you dearly love is being ruined ... and those hard working individuals, who wanted to make hmv great again, have mostly been fired, there seemed no other choice."

Eventually they gave a clue indicating that the management was on to them, when somebody tweeted: "Just overheard our

Marketing Director (he's staying, folks) ask 'How do I shut down Twitter?'"

Regrettably the management team could not do anything immediately to stop them as they did not seem to know the password to their Twitter account, as one of the tweets read: "Just overheard our Marketing Director (he's staying, folks!) ask 'How do I shut down Twitter?"

Furthermore, it was claimed that the official HMV account had been set up by an intern who volunteered for the company two years previously.

They were able to successfully post a few rebellious tweets before management was able to reclaim control of the Twitter account and erase the tweets.

Screenshots of some of the tweets can be seen below:-

The joint administrators for HMV failed to make any comments on the tweets, but confirmed that 190 redundancies were made across the company's head office and distribution network.

References

[1] http://www.dailymail.co.uk/news/article-2493662/Home-Depot-fires-racist-employee-tweet-African-American-drummers-gorilla.html

[2] http://www.cnet.com/uk/news/lg-mocks-apples-bent-iphone-but-uses-an-iphone-to-send-its-tweet/

[3] http://edition.cnn.com/2012/07/20/tech/social-media/nra-tweet-shooting/

[4] http://news.sky.com/story/1064801/luton-airport-sorry-over-crash-facebook-joke

[5]http://www.telegraph.co.uk/foodanddrink/foodanddrinknews/9810767/Horse-meat-scandal-Tesco-apologises-over-hay-Twitter-post.html

[6] http://www.dailymail.co.uk/news/article-2410058/Twitter-user-buys-promoted-tweet-criticise-British-Airwayss-service.html

[7] https://www.theguardian.com/business/2013/jan/31/hmv-workers-twitter-feed-sacking

Impact of Online Reputation on Recruitment

It goes without saying that the most valuable asset any company can have is good employees. More so, any organisation that wants to get ahead and make a head way will realise that they have to attract the best employees and also retain them. However, the reputation of an organisation can either attract or repel great employees.

There are numerous benefits that will accrue to employers that have positive online reputation. These include:

Attracting Top Talent

It is extremely easy to attract high quality candidates when you have a positive online reputation that is well publicised. A survey carried out by Glassdoor states that "69% would not take a job with a company that had a bad reputation, even if they were unemployed!" [1]

Low recruiting costs

Word will go round fast whenever there are vacancies in companies with positive reputation, as it would be a place where lots of people want to work. It will therefore be easy to recruit through word of mouth recommendations. Hence, the cost of recruiting will decrease because there will be no need for paid advertisements.

A research conducted by CareerBuilder confirms the view that recruitment costs will be low. The survey reveals that Job applicants " would accept a lower salary if the company had exceptionally positive reviews online (67 percent) or if the company had a lot of positive press recently (65 percent)." [2]

Talent retention

Companies with great reputation not only attract great talent, but they also retain them. Employee turnover will obviously be less in companies with good reputation.
The result of a survey conducted by Glassdoor confirms the above statement and it says "84% would consider leaving their current jobs if offered another role with a company that had an excellent corporate reputation." [3]

High recruitment costs

A company with a bad reputation will incur a high cost in order to both recruit and retain them. Glassdoor carried out a study whereby a number of people who were "currently employed, 58% said they would work at a company with a bad reputation, but it comes at a hefty price tag for the employer." It further reports that "25% said it would take more than a 50% pay raise, while 15% of respondents said their salary would have to more than double in order to work for the company with the bad reputation". [4]

Great reputation matters

It has been discovered that reputation has the tendency to carry more weight than money according to a study conducted by CareerBuilder. [5] The survey was as follows:- "when job seekers were asked if they would consider a salary that is 5 percent less than their lowest acceptable salary, a significant number said they would depending on the company's image and applicant experience". [5]

It is apparent that great company reputation attracts great talent, so work on your company reputation if you want the crème de la crème employees working for you.

Companies need to ensure that a key priority is having a good reputation in order to attract and compete for the best talent, especially when there is a shortage of skills.

References

[1] http://b2b-assets.glassdoor.com/50-hr-and-recruiting-stats.pdf

[2] http://www.careerbuilder.com/share/aboutus/pressreleasesdetail.aspx?sd=10%2f17%2f2013&siteid=cbpr&sc_cmp1=cb_pr785_&id=pr785&ed=12%2f31%2f2013

[3] http://b2b-assets.glassdoor.com/50-hr-and-recruiting-stats.pdf

[4] https://www.glassdoor.com/blog/companys-reputation-matters-bad-economy/

[5] http://www.careerbuilder.co.uk/share/aboutus/pressreleasesdetail.aspx?sd=10%2F17%2F2013&id=pr785&ed=12%2F31%2F2013

How to monitor your Online Reputation

The first thing you need to do regarding your reputation is to find out what state your reputation presently stands. When you search for your name or business name online the information that comes up on the first few search engine report pages (SERPs) will reveal what type of online reputation you have.

The best way therefore, is to start by assessing your online reputation is clearly by conducting searches on the major search engines - Google, Yahoo, AOL, Bing, etc.

It is vital to understand that there are two extremely noteworthy online reputation influences:

Organic search: This is the avenue that people use to locate you online, even if they do not know your business exists. Basically whatever is on the search results is what people will see and that is what will help them form an impression about your business and determine whether they buy from you or not.

Social media: This has a tremendous effect on your online reputation because every Facebook update, share or tweet bringing up your name shows up on Google search pages and these can have as much impact as your web pages.

It is therefore critical to assess your online reputation on a constant basis, especially on these two platforms. The way to do this is by taking the following steps:-

1. Search: The very first step to take is to conduct multiple organic searches online to find out what is being said about you. Indeed, the largest search engine is Google, however, it is essential to avoid focusing all of your searches on just one search engine. There are others that people use such as Yahoo!, Ask.com, Bing, and more.

When searching for your company, do more than just search for your name.

You need to search for at least the following:-

Your company name, brand name(s), product names and/or services. Your best bet is to enter your name in quotation marks so you can receive more targeted results.

Your company name with the city after the name.

Misspellings of your company name and different variations of spellings or misspellings of your company name.

Any usernames you use for your company on social media sites.

Any keywords or phrases that are closely linked to your business

The name of your brand in a good light, for example "best costume jewellery, High Trends Jewellery".

The name of your brand in a bad light, for example "worst costume jewellery, High Trends Jewellery".

Names of key personnel, such as CEO, Executive Directors and the like.

Be sure to search for the names people will actually use when searching for you.

Action Tip:
Set up a Google Alert for all the keywords that you search for so that you are notified anytime anything is published with those keywords. This will help you stay on top of your game and so will hardly be caught unawares about what is being said about you.

2. Use descriptive modifiers: There are some common terms that irate customers use when they want to leave negative reviews online. Ensure that you add those words to your company name when searching. Below are some examples of such words:

Sucks
Scam
Rip Off
Fraud
Complaint
Avoid
Beware of
Review

Type in your company name into the search engine and the phrases, for instance, "your company name + sucks" to get a list of results.

3. Related searches: Take note of the related searches that might come up at the bottom of the search results page. This could be useful in alerting you to some particular keywords people are using to look for your company online. The image below shows that "Your name" had been searched for and some phrases were generated at the bottom of the page that is related to "your name".

4. **Search anonymously:** Search engines tend to keep in depth records about you such as your location, language and so on. In order to get the most thorough results when you're conducting an assessment of your online reputation, make sure you log out of search engine accounts and disable personalised search. This will enable you see the same results that everyone else does. You should delete records of your past searches and browsing activities as well.

5.

Make sure you are not signed into any of your Google accounts when you are conducting this search.

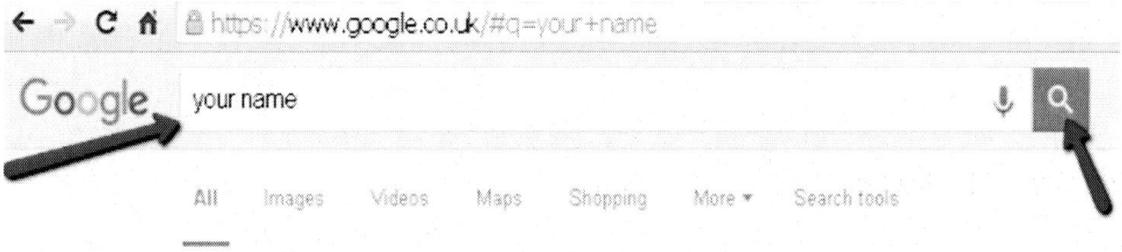

6. **Use multiple search engines:** Conduct your search on different search engines not just Google. You should also search on other major search engines such as Bing, Yahoo, AOL, Wow and Ask. It is a great idea to look beyond the first few pages of search results in order to get a good portrayal of your online reputation.

7. **Image and video searches:** Ensure that your searches include images and videos especially on Google as people do go ahead and search these two; they want to put a face to the name. As the saying goes "a picture is worth a thousand words"..... Ensure that what comes up on images and videos are great content.

8. Use metasearch engines:

According to Wikipedia, "a metasearch engine (or aggregator) is a search tool that uses another search engine's data to produce their own results from the Internet.[Metasearch engines take input from a user and simultaneously send out queries to third party search engines for results. Sufficient data is gathered, formatted by their ranks and presented to the users". [1]

Conduct searches on metasearch engines such as Dogpile, Ixquick and DuckDuckGo.

9. Social media platforms: Search for all your different products and names in their variations on social networking sites like Facebook, Google+, Twitter, YouTube, LinkedIn and more. It is in your best interest to search on as many social media platforms as possible. You are more likely to get more insights about what people think about your or your company when conducting social media searches than you would on search engines. The reality is that lots of people often talk about their experiences with businesses on social media platforms.

Action Tip:
Easily keep tabs with the mentions of your name on major social media sites by setting up a social media dashboard on a platform like Hootsuite. You will be able to access mentions of your name and any comments on top social sites such as Facebook, Twitter, LinkedIn, Google+, Instagram, YouTube, Pinterest and Tumblr.

10. Social bookmarking sites: You should also investigate social bookmarking websites such as StumbleUpon, Reddit and Delicious to see if there are any posts about you.

11. Review sites:

A review site is a forum where reviews can be posted about companies, products, services and even people. Review sites are becoming more accepted as they are increasingly being used by the buying community as the "go to" place to find out people's experiences regarding products and services.

Business review sites give potential customers the opportunity to gain information your business and afford you the chance to display your satisfied customers. It is therefore of the utmost importance to offer excellent customer service so you can receive positive reviews.

A review site is another great place to retrieve information about your online reputation, some examples of review sites are Angie's List, Insider Pages, Merchant Circle, Trustpilot, TripAdvisor and other similar sites. Users are able to leave reviews for products and services for everyone to read. A lot of online shoppers go to these sites to see what reviews have been left before taking the final step to patronise your business. Review sites are very instrumental in transforming potential customers to actual customers.

Action Tip:

Set up a reviews page on your website and post all your positive reviews there. This will make it easy for potential customers looking for reviews about your business to come across them and it will help them make up their minds about doing business with you.

Insider Pages
www.insiderpages.com

Merchant Circle
www.merchantcircle.com

Angieslist
www.angieslist.com

Trustpilot
www.trustpilot.com

TripAdvisor
www.tripadvisor.co.uk

12. Local Listings: A local business listing is a platform online where you can list your details such as business name, address, phone number, etc. There are a number such directories where business owners can set up free business listings.

Customers tend to leave reviews on these sites, so special attention should be paid to them. You should be sure to check all the major listings to see what is being said about you. It is also important that you claim, verify and optimise your local listings if you have not done that already. This will give you control over your listings.

Mentioned below are some very influential listings that you should monitor:-

Google My Business
http://www.google.com/business

Google My Business is definitely the most important listing to be on by virtue of the fact that Google is the biggest search engine in the world at the moment. This dashboard is likely to be where most customers will leave reviews. It is Google's most recent local business listing directory/review site. It replaces Google Places and Google+ Local and is a combination of the two. It is imperative that you access this dashboard frequently to check and respond to customer reviews.

Make sure you claim, verify and optimise your Google My Business listing, so that you can have some control over the reviews on it.

Go to: http://www.google.com/business/ and follow the steps accordingly.

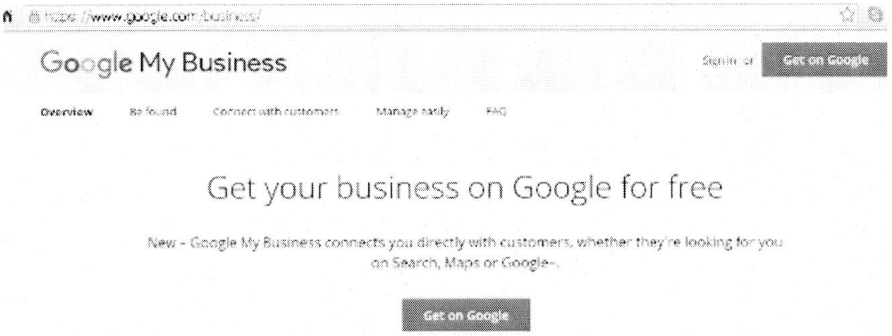

Yelp

www.yelp.com

Yelp is the next most significant site to monitor as many local customers go there to both leave reviews about local companies and also to read reviews about businesses they are contemplating doing business with.

Make sure you claim, verify and optimise your Yelp listing, so that you can have some control over the reviews on it.

Go to: https://biz.yelp.com/ and enter your company's name and the city where it is located.

Locate your business from the list that comes up and then click on the "Claim This Business" link to the right and follow the necessary steps to complete.

Yahoo Local

This is another really important local listing site that must be monitored and if your listing has not been claim, ensure you claim it.

Yahoo Local is now **Aabaco Small Business**
https://www.aabacosmallbusiness.com/local-listings

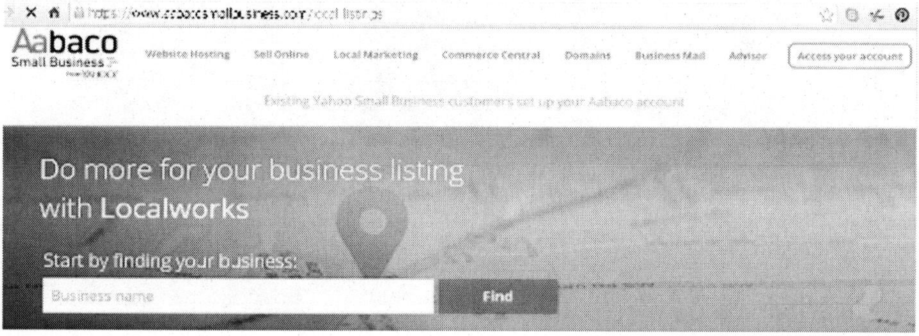

Bing Local

https://www.bingplaces.com

CitySearch

www.citysearch.com

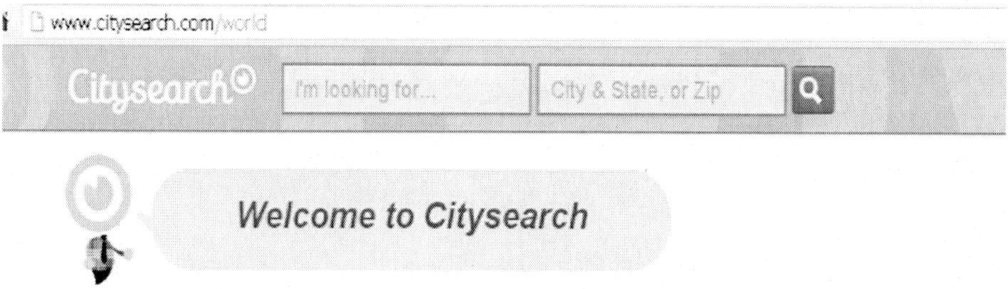

Foursquare
www.business.foursquare.com

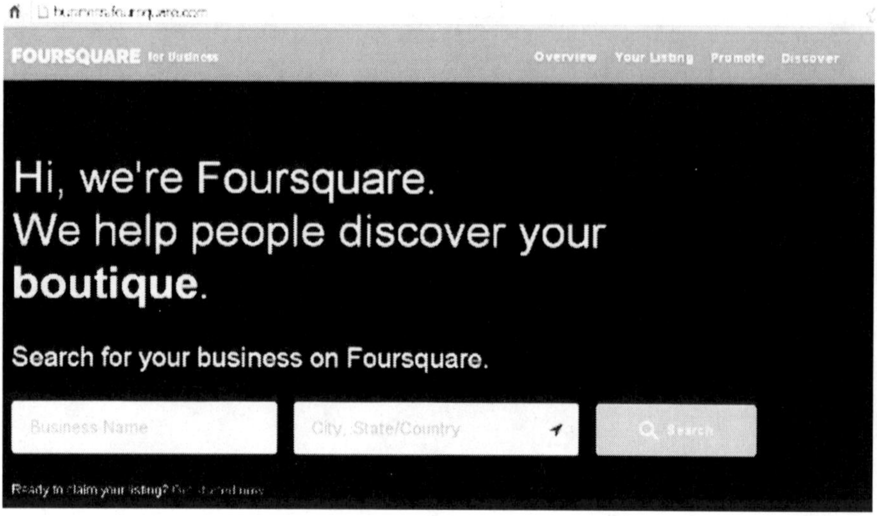

12. Search Complaint Websites

"Complaint" websites have been set up explicitly to provide an avenue for consumers share their bad experiences when they feel that they have gotten a bad deal, or have been cheated, conned, defeated etc. Search such websites to see if there are any unfavourable and negative comments about your business.

Below are some of the important complaint websites:

www.ripoffreport.com

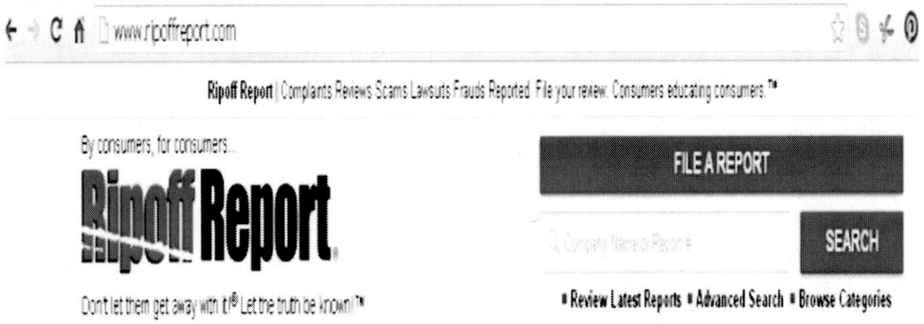

www.complaints.com

www.pissedconsumer.com

www.complaintsboard.com

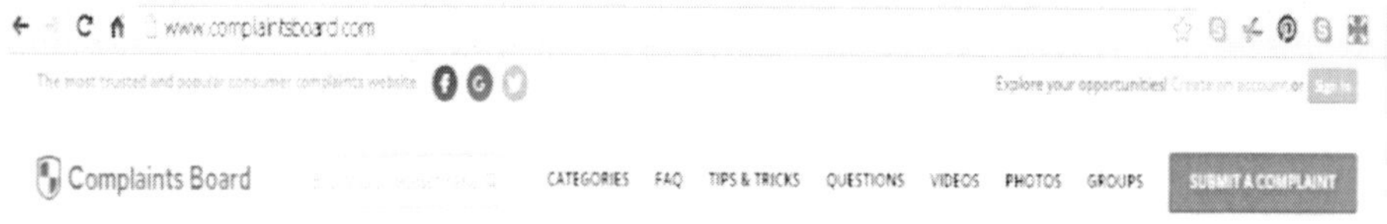

www.shamscam.com

www.customerservicescoreboard.com

13. Search the Better Business Bureau Website www.bbb.org

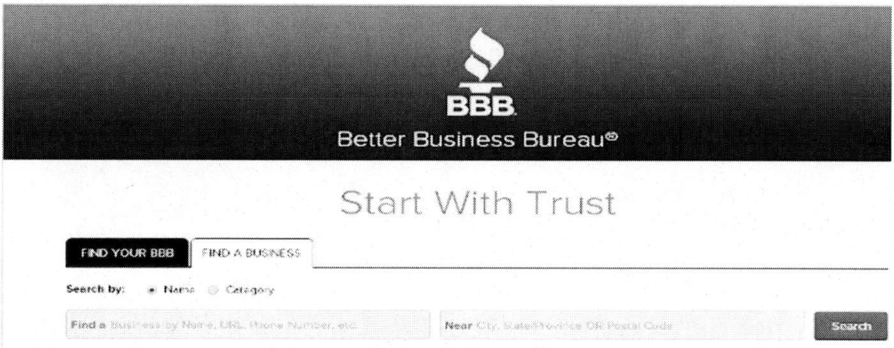

The BBB is "dedicated to fostering honest and responsive relationships between businesses and consumers -- instilling consumer confidence and advancing a trustworthy marketplace for all" [2].

This is another platform that potential customers check out when companies they are deliberating on which companies to do business with.
All you have to do is go to BBB.com, type in your city and state, you will be directed to the local BBB site and then search for your company's which should reveal your rating, reasons for the ratings and a summary of customer complaints.

Another way of conducting the search is by 'Googling' "your company name + bbb" and the results will come up on the search results if there are records of your company on that site.

14. **Industry forums and blogs:** This is another vital source of information as one negative review on a leading industry forum or blog can certainly have an adverse effect on your reputation.

Action Tip:
Monitor and respond to both comments that you have made on third party blogs as well as comments on your blog posts. You will be notified of such comments on most blogging platforms; the onus is however on you to respond accordingly. Ensure you comment on posts that you have been mentioned in that you did not create, that way you will be able to opt for additional comment notifications. This will enable you to continue to be part of the conversation.

15. Quora: These are social media platforms where people can ask questions about any topic and get responses from members of the community. These are great sources of information and a number of companies are active on Quora in particular, answering questions on the site and this helps them improve their reputation.

References

[1] https://en.wikipedia.org/wiki/Metasearch_engine
[2]https://www.bbb.org/council/about

Online Reputation Assessment

You will do well to use the information above to assess your current online reputation. This enable you to determine where you are at and help you work out what steps you need to take based on the results.

You need to track and record the search results that you come up with. The Assessment Spreadsheet below is a very valuable tool to use when conducting a search for the relevant keywords or phrases on the pertinent search engines. You can log the top fifty search results on it.

Assessment Worksheet
Search Engine:__________ Phrase Searched:__________
Date: ____

Pages*	URL	Type*	Comments*
1			
2			
3			
4			
5			

***Pages** – Conduct searches on at least the first five pages of the search engines. However, you can choose to extend your search beyond these pages.

***Type** – Record the type of search result being displayed – is it something on a website, blog post, social media post, review site, directory, local listing, image, video, etc.

***Comments** – Record your findings - positive, negative or indifferent and whether it is about you as an individual, your employees, brand, product or your company. Ensure that you record it. if it has anything remotely to do with you.

Reputation Evaluation

Ideally, your self-search should reveal at the very least, that you are directly influence the first pages of the search engines. You need to take a step further by collating and evaluating the results you got. Record how many were positive, bad, indifferent and how many showed up under your name that had absolutely no relevance to you. This information will give you a clear indication of what you need to do about your online reputation.

However, there are no specific rules defining "positive" or "negative" online reputation, this is to give you an indication about where there is room for improvement.

The positive comments and posts online about you will be apparent and so will majority of the adverse publicity that you discover.

Positive Results

If the results you have are positive – great! However, you should not rest on your laurels, you need to keep building on this and also keep monitoring your reputation. There are many a companies that started with good reputations, took it for granted, focussed on other stuff and then later found out that whilst their attention was somewhere else, situations and circumstances occurred that led to their reputations being tarnished, so they lost what they had. In addition, it is to you advantage if you are in control of most of the results that shows up online about you, it could be sites like some of your social media platforms, your blog, verified local listing an so forth.

Negative Results

If the results are negative, you have your work cut out for you. It is important to deal with this issue as a matter of great urgency. Some companies have been completely wiped out because of their negative online reputation. It is also extremely unwise to think that the issue will resolve itself or go away, as this is rarely the case when it comes to negative online reputation. The reality of it is, if prompt action is not taken the issue actually gets worse. In a lot of instances professional help is needed to resolve this.

Results

When consumers, shareholders, employers, the media, etc are seeking information about you, you want them to find relevant and positive results. If the search results are crowded with indifferent Web sites detailing competitive research and company profiles, the user isn't finding something that immediately wins them over. It's to be expected that you'll have a Wikipedia entry if you're a big business, or a directory listing, but if that's the majority of your search presence, how is the information gatherer supposed to build a positive impression of you? They've simply recognized that there's nothing glaringly wrong.

Irrelevant or Zero Results

If none of the search results in the first page for your name or company are related to you then that is an issue that needs to be resolved urgently as well. This is because this makes it possible for anyone to easily ruin your reputation online, as whatever they post online about your name or company will get to the first page without any problems..

However, if you share a name with a celebrity, a high profile personality or huge company, this might not necessarily be the case, as it can be pretty difficult to rank on the first page of the search engines if you have those as your competition. The truth is that, at the end of the day people will still want expect to locate you online. It is up to you to ensure that you find a way to ensure that you are available.

Having said that, if you find nothing at all about yourself on the search engines then it means that you are on ground zero - you do not exist and so have to start from the scratch to build your online reputation.

Level of Relevance of Results

It is also paramount to evaluate the level of relevance of the search engine results as this will give you a clue as to how much work you need to do on you online reputation.

Zero relevance – This will indicate that the search engine results that come up have absolutely no relevance to you at all or does not display how you want to be known.

Slight relevance - A small number of the results displayed portrays how you want to be known.

Partial relevance – This is when approximately 50% of what is online expresses how you want to be known.

Significant relevance – In this instance about 75% of what is online is what you want displayed.

Total relevance – Nearly 100% of the results displayed truly reflects what you want displayed.

Statistics Supporting Businesses Monitoring Reputation

It is important to have a great online reputation which will be mainly fueled by individuals' reviews, comments, posts etc. online. The opinions of people carry a lot of weight. Potential customers looking online at business reviews highly value the feedback of people they can relate to – people just like themselves. This observation was corroborated by PR mega-firm Edelman in their 2007 Trust Barometer. (Edelman) 2007 Trust Barometer Findings.[1]

The findings are as follows:-
52% of people that undertook a survey from developed nations said someone they consider to be "a person like yourself" would provide the most reliable information. (Edelman)2007 Trust Barometer Findings. [1]
The Edelman findings go on to say that "in the European Union, North America, and Latin America, "a person like me" is considered the most credible deliverer of information about a company. In Asia, "a person like me" is second to physicians". (Edelman)2007 Trust Barometer Findings.[1]

The Edelman findings has been highlighted in the diagram below [2]:-

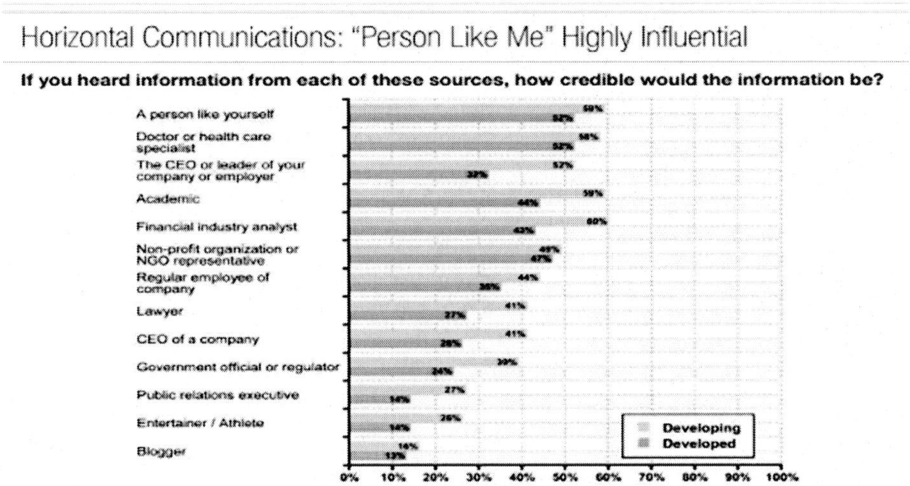

The Edelman findings about credible markets has been highlighted in the diagram below [3]:-

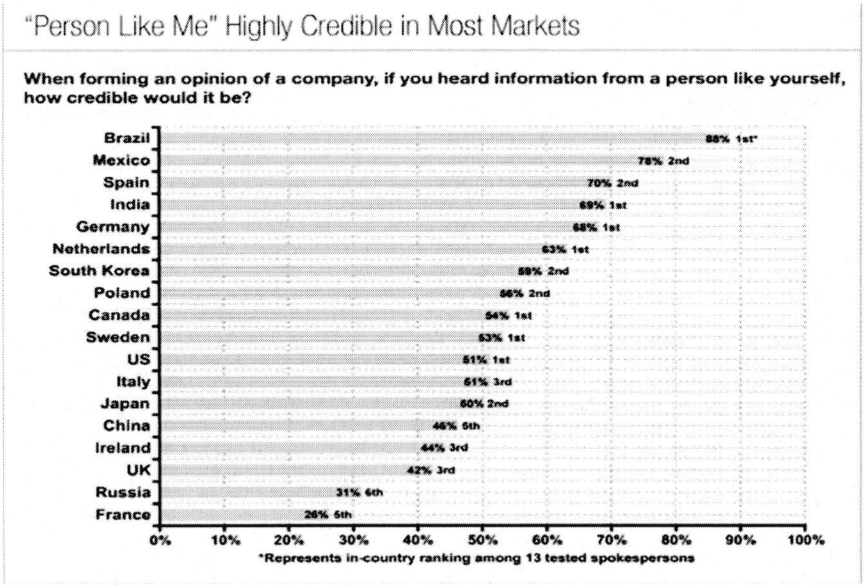

Other people's experiences

An increasing number of people share their purchase experiences. A survey conducted by Zendesk disclosed that 58% more people today will tell others about their customer services experiences than five years ago. [Zendesk] [4]

The survey go on to reveal that more people - 45% share bad customer service experiences than those that will share good customer service experiences - 30%, via social media. [Zendesk] [4]

According to a report compiled by Nielsen in 2012, a high percentage of people 70% go online to find out other people's experiences and 50% will share their concerns/complaints about businesses online. [5]

The diagram [5] below details the findings of the report:-

Social Care

The Nielsen report [6] also reveals that "47% of Social Media Users engage in Social Care" (Social Care in this context, can be described as a form of Customer Service on Social Media) see diagram [6] below:-

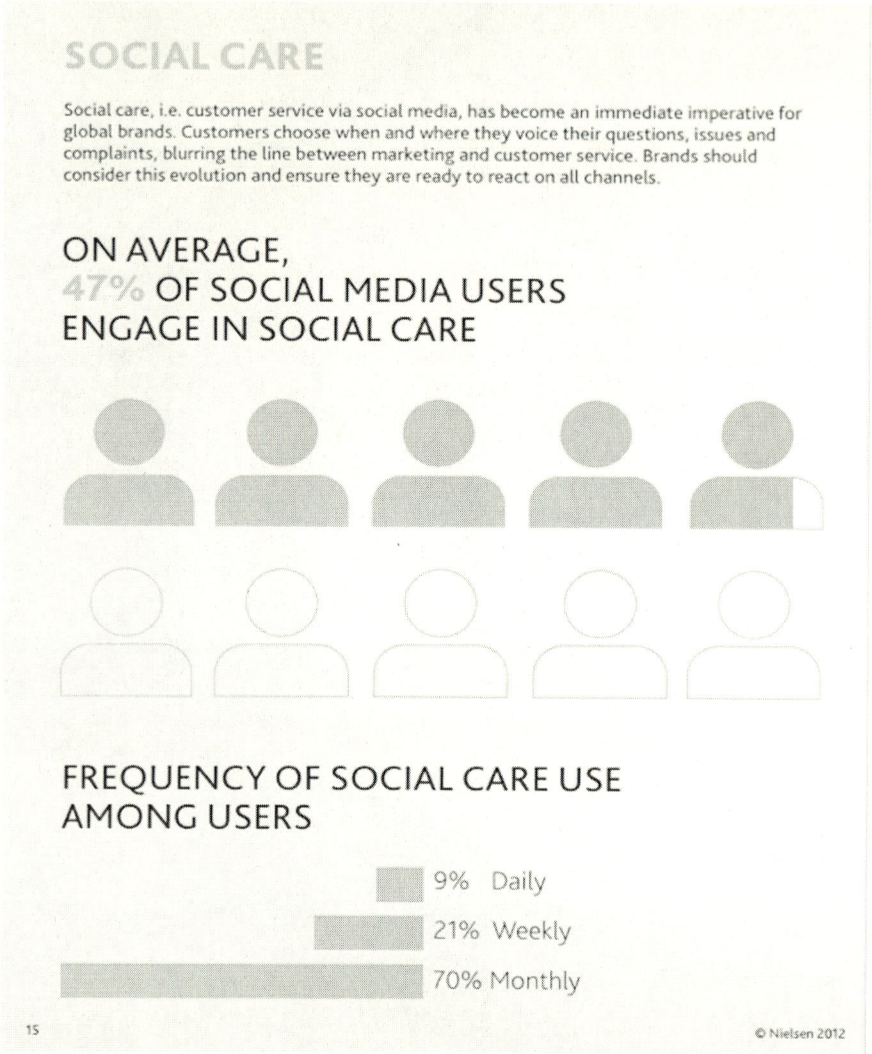

The diagram [7] below discloses that one third of social media users have a preference for social care above phoning companies.

Word-of-mouth recommendations

With the proliferation of social media these days, it so easy for people to connect with the friends and family and find out what is going on with them as well as know what their opinions are about products and services. It is therefore easy to get word-of-mouth recommendations from friends and family, and this is the most influential form of advertising according to a report by Nielsen published in September 2013, 84% of people surveyed online across 58 countries said this source was the most credible. [8]

Online consumer opinions

68% of people surveyed pointed out that they trust opinions of consumers posted online. This number actually increased by 7% in 2013 from when the survey was done in 2007. [8]

Global Average - Percent of Completely/Somewhat Trust

FORM OF ADVERTISING	2013	2007	DIFFERENCE 2013 VS. 2007
Recommendations from people I know	84%	78%	6%
Branded websites	69%	60%	9%
Consumer opinions posted online	68%	61%	7%
Editorial content such as newspaper articles	67%	*	*
Ads on TV	62%	56%	6%
Brand sponsorships	61%	49%	12%
Ads in newspapers	61%	63%	-2%
Ads in magazines	60%	56%	4%
Billboards and other outdoor advertising	57%	*	*
Ads on radio	57%	54%	3%
Emails I signed up for	56%	49%	7%
Ads before movies	56%	38%	18%
TV program product placements	55%	*	*
Ads served in search engine results	48%	34%	14%
Online video ads	48%	*	*
Ads on social networks	48%	*	*
Display ads on mobile devices	45%	*	*
Online banner ads	42%	26%	16%
Text ads on mobile phones	37%	18%	19%

*Not included in Nielsen 2007 Global Survey.
Source: Nielsen Global Survey of Trust in Advertising, Q3 2007 and Q1 2013

nielsen AN UNCOMMON SENSE OF THE CONSUMER™

The result of this survey can be seen in the diagram [8] below:-

The result of a survey conducted by Forrester of more than 58,000 respondents was published in March, 2013 and it revealed that 70% of "US online adults trust brand or product recommendations from friends and family and 46% trust consumer-written online reviews, while just 10% trust ads on websites and 9% trust text messages from companies or brands". [9]

Points of influence

Google joined forces with TNS and Ogilvy [10] to carry out a six-month survey, they interviewed almost 2,500 consumers that had recently bought goods in the auto, beauty and smartphone categories. The key findings are below:

Word of mouth (74%)
Retailers and store visits (69%)
You Tube – how-to videos, product visualisation, entertainment (64%)
Twitter (61%)
Company/brand websites (59%)
Facebook (56%)
Pinterest (56%)
Newspapers and magazines (55%)
TV and movies (51%)
Search (51%)

These figures have been transferred onto the diagram [11] below:-

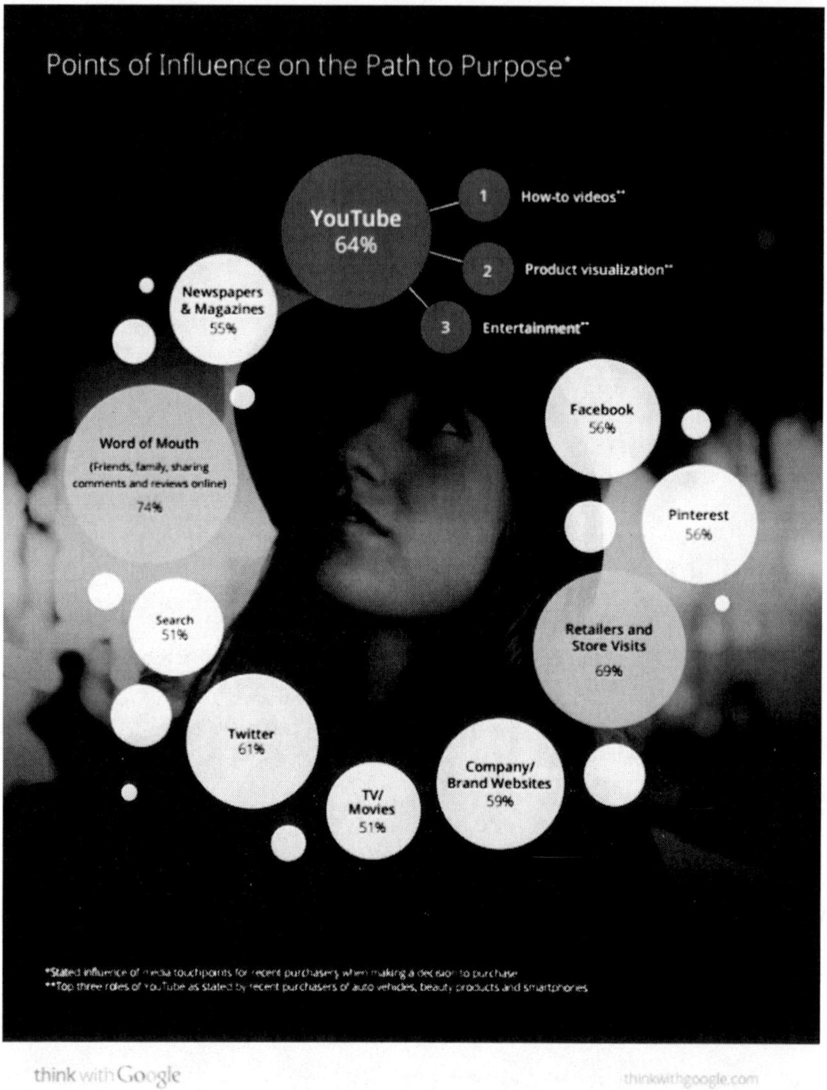

Search Engines

As more and more people are going online to look for information in order to make decisions regarding the business they will patronise, it is imperative that what the
search engines conjure up are flattering. In most cases what they do is type the name of the company they are considering

doing business with, into the search engines and they tend to believe the results the search engines bring up.

According to the 2015 Edelman Trust Barometer, search engines have become the "most trusted source for general news and information among the informed public, surpassing traditional media by two percentage points among the global informed public, and by eight percentage points among Millennials".[12]

The diagram [12] below illustrates this point:-

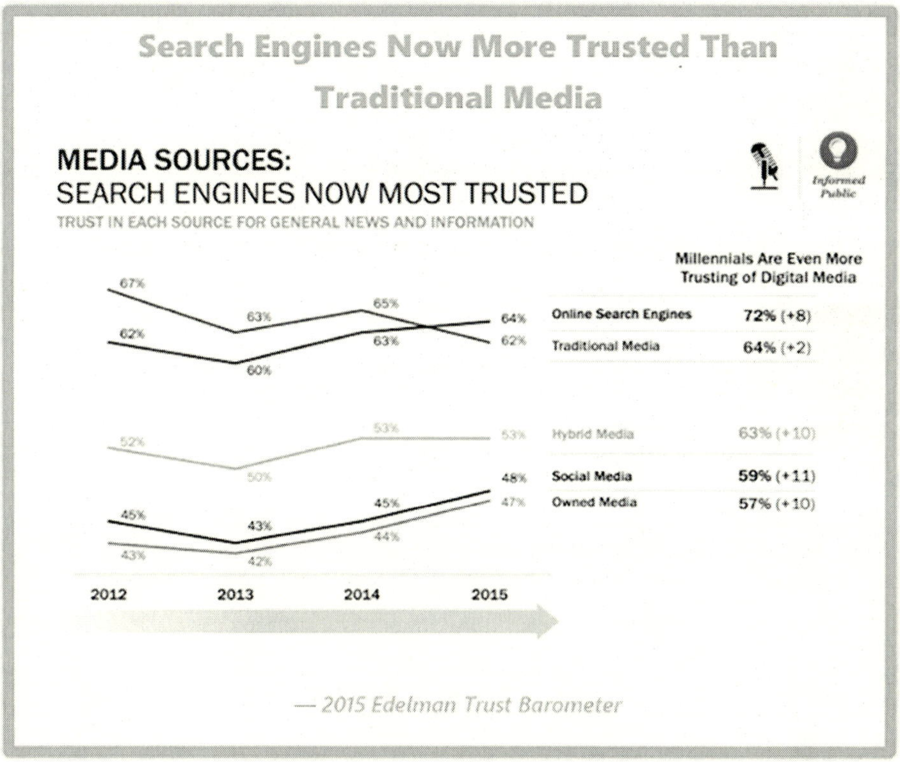

Review sites

The impact of online reviews on buyer decisions is on the increase. A survey conducted by Zendesk asking if they had seen reviews online about customer service, the response was that "about two-thirds of participants (63% for negative and 69% for positive) reported that they did recall reading these online reviews". [13]

Negative reviews about customer service (39%) were most commonly seen on review sites and positive reviews of customer service (44%) were mostly found on Facebook. [13] The diagram [13] below from Zendesk illustrates the findings about online reviews:-

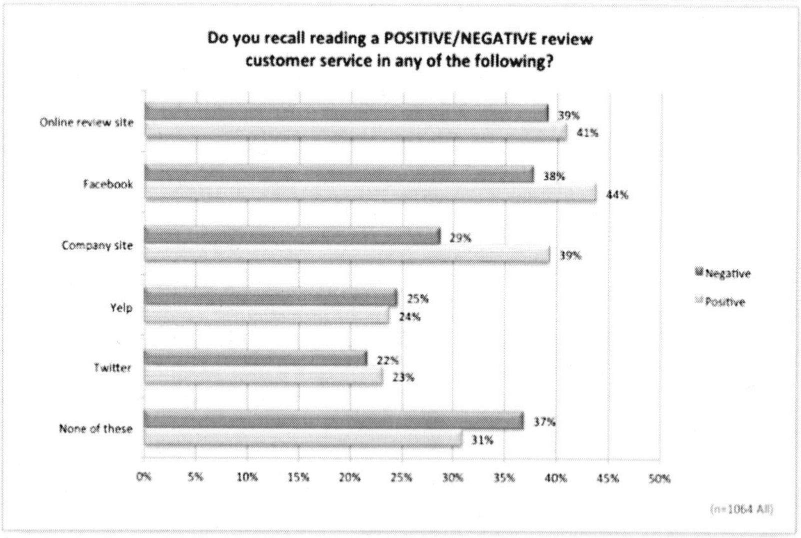

Majority of the people who did the survey who had seen reviews professed that the information influenced their buying decisions. "This was true of both positive reviews (90%) as well as negative reviews (86%)". [13]The diagram below illustrates this:-

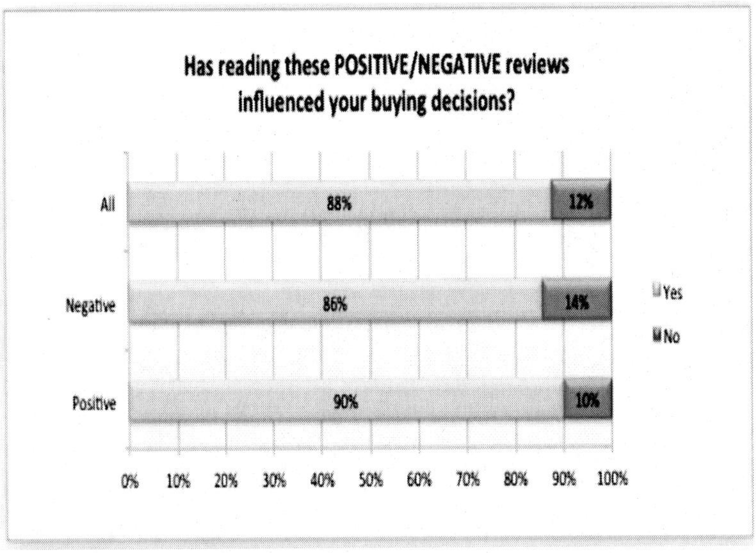

Customer Service Interactions

Customers tend to share more of their bad customer experiences than the good.
The partakers of the Zendesk survey confirmed this when they indicated that they shared "stories about bad customer service (95%) than told about good experiences (87%)". They also recounted a wide use of social media "(45% for bad and 30% for good) and online review sites (35% for bad and 23% for good) to spread stories about customer service experiences". [13]

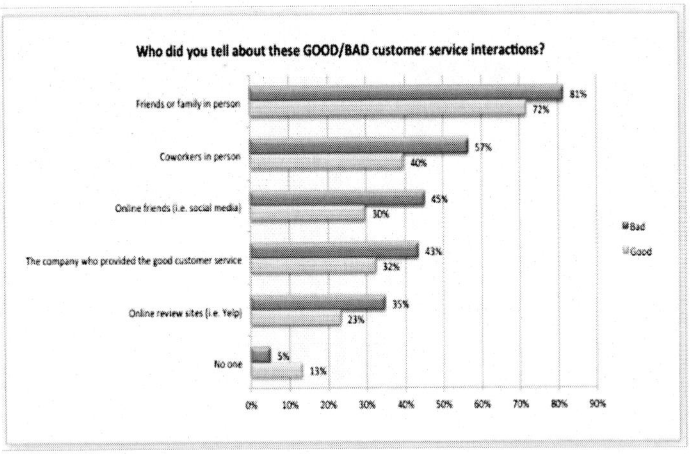

Social Media Influence

The Institute of Customer Service conducted a survey, the results were published in the Guardian in May 2015 [14] and one of the main conclusions is that “consumers are turning to social media to communicate with brands at a rapid rate.”

The following are also some of the results of the survey:-

- Customer complaints made on social media had increased eight-fold since January 2014.
- 25% of social media users in the UK have complained on the platform in the previous three months.
- Platforms such as Twitter and Facebook are increasingly being seen as the best means for customers to intensify complaints.
- 12% of the 2,195 survey participants had done this in the past. This was considered an easy, inexpensive and expedient way to log complaints.
- 31% of people using social media make pre-sales enquiries through it. (Institute of Customer Service). [14]

The above statistics demonstrates that potential customers and recruiters are increasingly researching individuals and business online before recruiting or procuring products and/or services from them. It is quite clear therefore that the success of your business is highly impacted by what customers say about you online.

References

[1] https://www.edelman.com/assets/uploads/2014/01/2007-Trust-Barometer-Executive-Summary.pdf Pg6
[2] https://www.edelman.com/assets/uploads/2014/01/2007-Trust-Barometer-Executive-Summary.pdf Pg7
[3] https://www.edelman.com/assets/uploads/2014/01/2007-Trust-Barometer-Executive-Summary.pdf Pg9
[4] https://www.zendesk.com/resources/customer-service-and-lifetime-customer-value
[5]http://www.nielsen.com/content/dam/corporate/us/en/reports-downloads/2012-Reports/The-Social-Media-Report-2012.pdf pg20
[6]http://www.nielsen.com/content/dam/corporate/us/en/reports-downloads/2012-Reports/The-Social-Media-Report-2012.pdf pg15
[7]http://www.nielsen.com/content/dam/corporate/us/en/reports-downloads/2012-Reports/The-Social-Media-Report-2012.pdf pg16
[8]http://www.nielsen.com/us/en/insights/news/2013/under-the-influence-consumer-trust-in-advertising.html
[9]https://www.forrester.com/How+Branded+Content+Will+Unlock+The+Key+To+Consumer+Trust/-/E-PRE4784
[10] http://think.storage.googleapis.com/docs/the-path-to-purpose_articles.pdf pg1
[11] http://think.storage.googleapis.com/docs/the-path-to-purpose_articles.pdf pg6
[11] https://www.zendesk.com/resources/customer-service-and-lifetime-customer-value/
[12] http://www.edelman.com/post/intellectual-property-trust-age-digital-media/
[13] https://www.zendesk.co.uk/resources/customer-service-and-lifetime-customer-value/
[14] http://www.theguardian.com/media-network/2015/may/21/customer-complaints-social-media-rise

Monitoring Tools

Do you take heed of what is being said about you online?

It takes time, effort and an elaborate strategy to build a solid company reputation, but everything you have worked hard to build can be undone in a matter of just a few hours. Negativity spreads like wildfire, especially in an environment that is open 24/7. Any online content, positive or negative, impacts how people view your business.

Monitoring your reputation is vital since anyone can post any information online regardless of whether it is true or not. Unfortunately, customers who are happy about the service they received will seldom write about it, while dissatisfied customers will tell everyone and also leave negative feedback. That is why it is imperative that you keep abreast of what is being said about you and monitor online dialogues.

Sporadically looking for the name of your company is not adequate. It is always better to begin to manage your online reputation before problems arise. It is advisable to be proactive about taking charge of your online reputation, do not leave it to chance. The magnitude and complexity of the Internet coupled with the speed at which news travels means it is difficult to continuously monitor all that is being said. To tackle this problem, you need an early warning system to alert you of all news relating to your brand, so you may remedy when needed.

There are a number of monitoring tools that can be used that will notify you whenever you are mentioned online whether in a good or bad context. You can use them to find out the conversations going on about your competitors' and any other information that is of interest to you.

Below are some social monitoring tools available that to do the work for you.

1. Google Alerts

When you set up Google alerts you will basically receive email alerts each time anyone mentions your company or whatever name you are tracking. Google Alerts lets you set up keyword searches for your company name or even your competition, if you want to keep tabs on what they are doing. You will receive instant updates through email daily or weekly directly into your inbox or through an RSS feed.

It is extremely easy to set up. Simply go to www.google.com/alerts and fill out your company name search query. You can select which type of content you are looking for, your preferred update frequency and quantity. Google Alerts will update you and keep you informed about new mentions on the web.

Make sure you add a very specific search query and select the appropriate channel; otherwise you will end up receiving too many alerts in your email inbox.
See below:

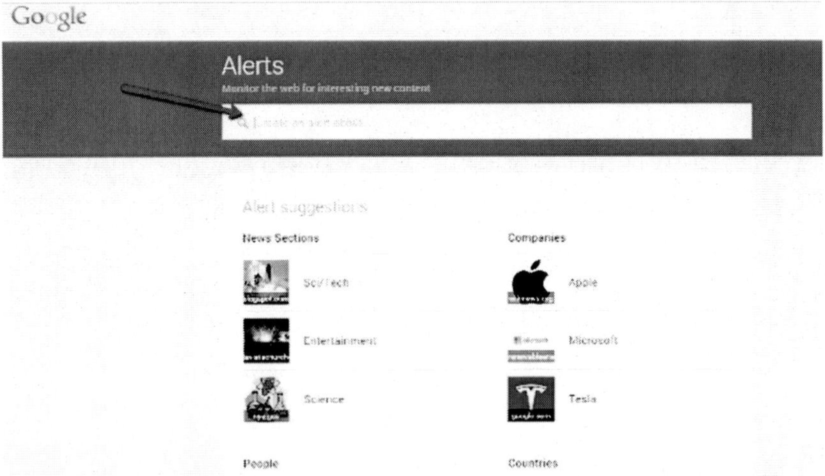

This is where your preferences will be selected, such as:

How Often – You can choose - once per day, once per week, or as-it-happens, whatever suits you best. Bear in mind that these alerts will be sent into the Google email account linked to your Alerts.

Sources – Select what you want to be alerted about, be it news, videos, etc. If you want to be notified about everything, it is recommended that you choose the "Automatic" option.

Language and Region – This is quite clear, input your preferred language and region for the alert.

How Many – Indicate "Only the best results" if you are after high quality, related terms. Select "All results" if that is your preference, this will include low quality ones.

Deliver To – You choose where you want to view your alerts either through RSS feed or your linked Google email account.

Alert Suggestions –Under the "Alert suggestions" section, Google will bring up other suggestions, simply click on the "+" next to them if you want to add them and they will be added to your alert list.

Once all of your preferences have been chosen, you can click on the "Create Alert" button at the bottom.

2. Tweet Alarm

Twitter is huge so it is important to monitor your name on Twitter, according to internetlivestats.com, "every second, on average, around 6,000 tweets are tweeted on Twitter, which corresponds to over 350,000 tweets sent per minute, 500 million tweets per day and around 200 billion tweets per year". http://www.internetlivestats.com/twitter-statistics/

Tweet Alarm is a great automatic monitoring system to use keep updated on what happens on Twitter. Tweet alarm will alert you by send you email whenever someone tweets about your brand, products or anything that interests you. Registration is required.

3. TweetBeep

TweetBeep works in a similar manner to Google Alerts, the only difference being that it monitors your reputation exclusively on Twitter. A free version of Tweetbeep will send you updates every hour whenever you are mentioned on Twitter.

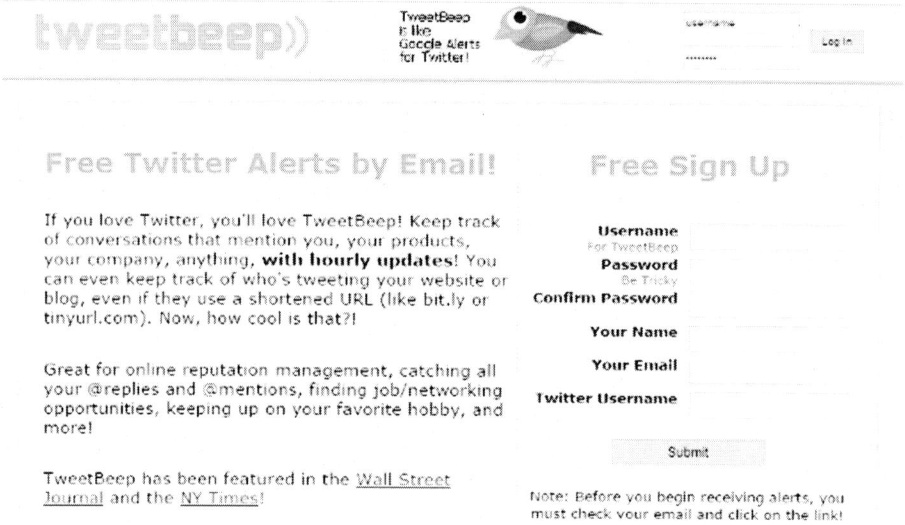

4. HootSuite

HootSuite is a popular tool that can be used for enhancing and managing multiple social media accounts such as Facebook, Twitter, MySpace, Google+ Pages, LinkedIn, WordPress, Foursquare etc from one location. HootSuite eradicates the time consuming element involved in managing several social media accounts. It helps in monitoring what is being said about you and enables you to give immediate responses. It also amongst a number of other benefits makes it possible for you to schedule messages in advance from all your social media channels and post updates or respond directly.

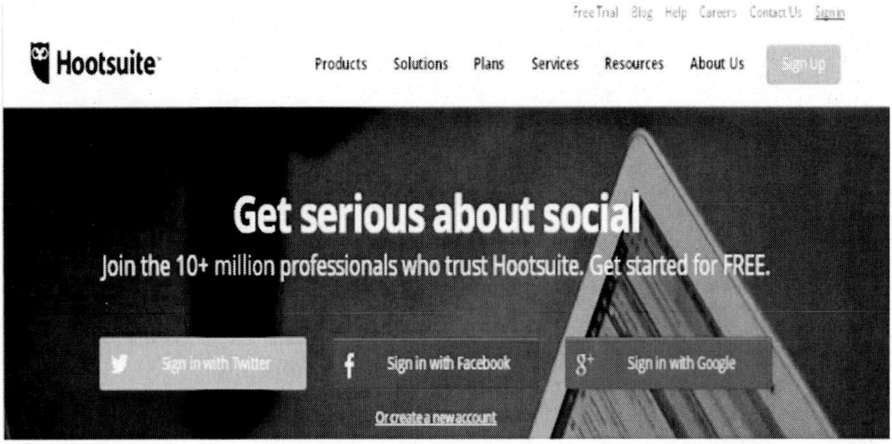

5. Social Mention

What Social Mention does according to the website [1] is that, "it allows you to easily track and measure what people are saying about you, your company, a new product, or any topic across the web's social media landscape in real-time. Social Mention monitors 100+ social media properties directly including: Twitter, Facebook, FriendFeed, YouTube, Digg, Google etc."

Social Mention enables you to see whether your company started off any dialogues on social media, what the author/mention ratio is, what your influence score is and people's sentiment.

It assists in tracking blogs, blog comments, mainstream news, Twitter, images, audio and video.

6. Mention

This is an iPhone and Android app that allows you to set up alerts for your company, brand, keywords, and your competition. 'Mention' has a number of features, it allows you to "connect social accounts to your alerts and react without leaving the application". In addition it helps you "monitor millions of sources in 42 languages and make sure you're not missing anything published on social networks, news sites, forums, blogs or any web page". [2]

7. Whos Talkin

This is a social media search tool that displays what is being said about you on different social networks. It is a simple tool to use, you basically enter the name of your company, click search and wait for the results. Whos Talkin will not help you manage the results, but will let you know pretty quickly what is being said about you online. You now have to make a decision on what you do with the results.

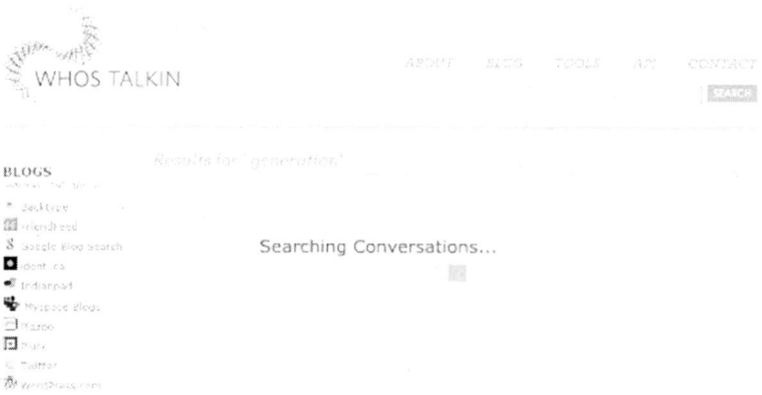

8. Cyfe

Cyfe is an all-in-one dashboard software that helps you monitor and analyze data scattered across all your online services like Google Analytics, Salesforce, AdSense, MailChimp, Facebook, WordPress and more from one single location in real-time

9. Technorati

This is one of the main blog search engine directories. You can use this for blog posts monitoring as well as to search for keywords connected to your company and even your competition.

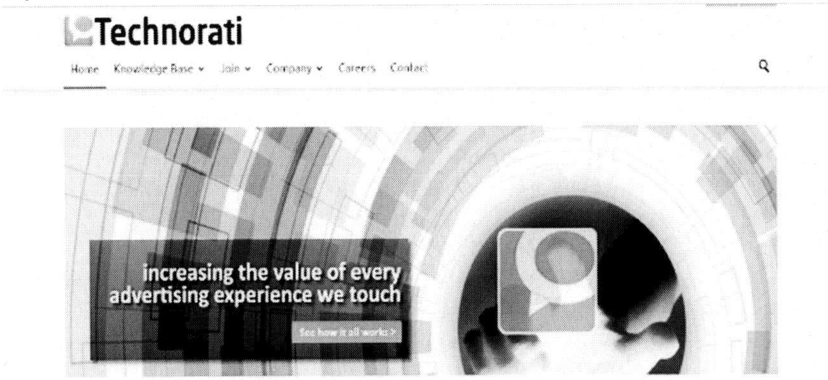

10. "Addictomatic searches the best live sites on the web for the latest news, blog posts, videos and images. It's the perfect tool to keep up with the hottest topics, perform ego searches and feed your addiction for what's up, what's now or what other people are feeding on". [3]

This tool summarises on one page how your brand is being perceived on a variety of social media platforms.

11. Pin Alerts

Pin Alerts will send emails to inform you when your website gets a new pin on Pinterest. This service can be set up very quickly and easily. Once set up automatic notifications will be sent this is great as users do not have to continuously monitor the pins. The users dictate how often they want to receive the email alerts, be it in real time as it happens, daily or weekly. The emails will include a link to the latest pins and description. Pin Alerts has the ability to track more than one domain.

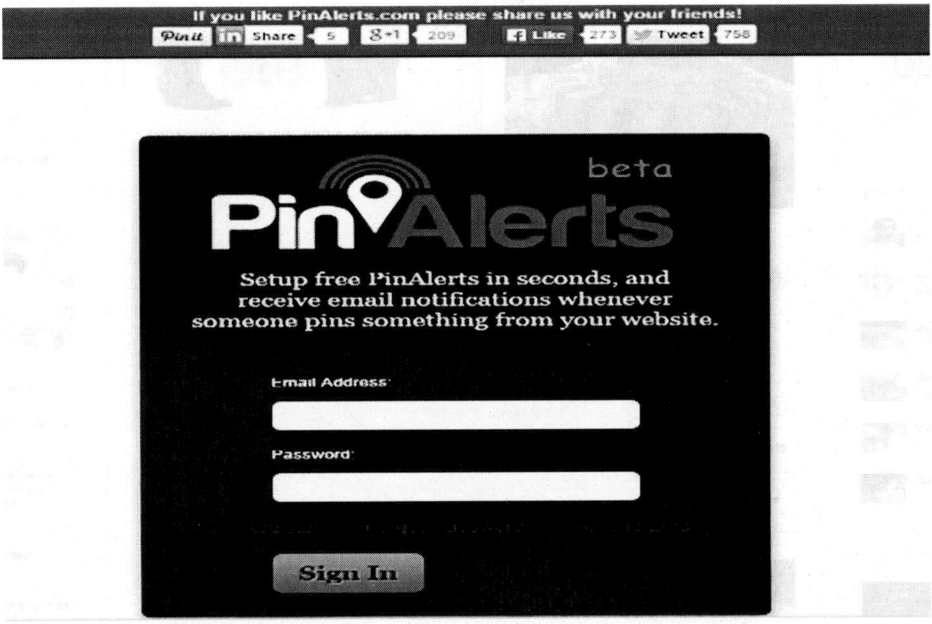

12. Topsy

This is a great social analytics tool that you can use to scan the internet to find mentions of your company name, product, competition etc. The main thing that makes this tool different from the other monitoring tools is that it has indexed every single tweet that has ever been tweeted.

Topsy does not only let you find out about what is being said about you online, but also reveal trending topics that you can include on your dashboard.

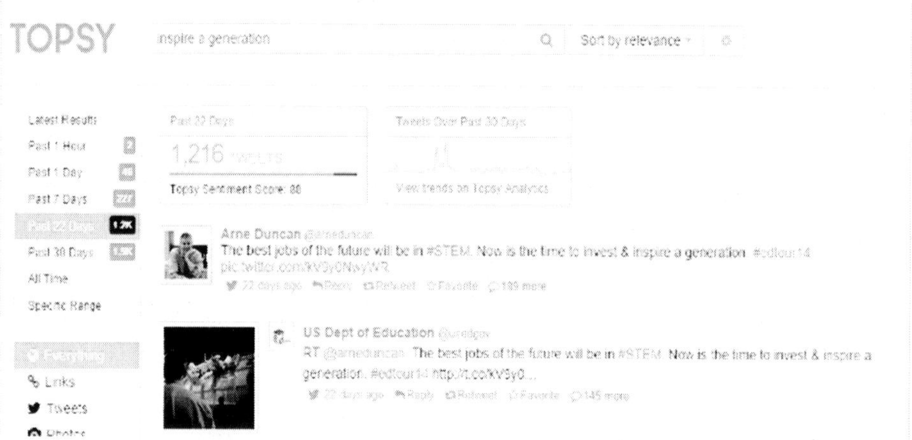

13. If This Then That

If This Then That, is a fairly new social media tool that enables you to "put the internet to work for you". It helps you connect with numerous social media platforms and devices, so that you generate so-called "recipes", this will help you get notifications. "Most Personal Recipes check for new Trigger data every 15 minutes, some are even faster". In addition you can choose one of the public recipes and reproduce what some other people are doing on this platform.

14. Netvibes

Netvibes is an all-in-one dashboard intelligence platform that you can use for social media monitoring in real-time. You do not have to be online to read feeds, this can be done anywhere including offline. Netvibes can be used on different devices such as iPhone, iPad, Android, desktop browser etc.

15. Image Raider

Image Raider is a tool that you can use to detect if someone is using your photo online. All you do is upload your photo on Image Raider and it will conduct a reverse image search and let you know if there are people talking about you using your pictures without saying your name. It will also enable you discover if your photos have been stolen or altered.

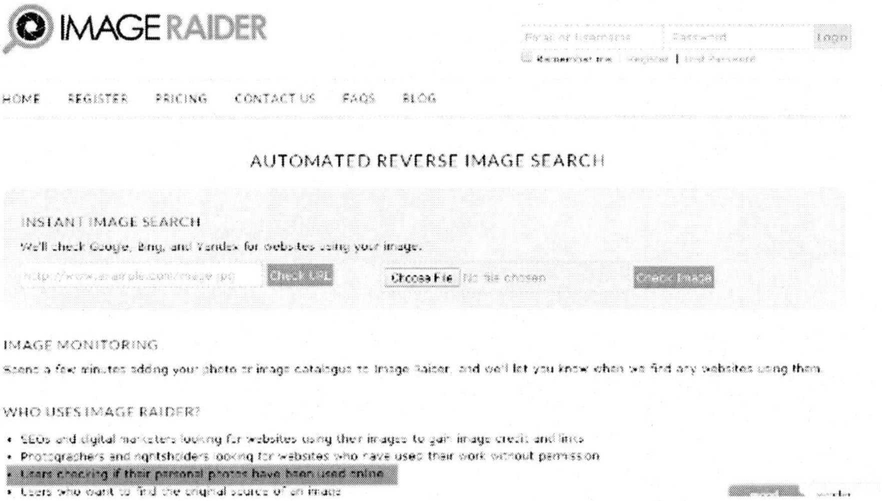

16. Icerocket

Icerocket is a tool that you can use to monitor mentions of your company online be it on blogs, Facebook and Twitter. It is relatively easy to use all you do is type what you want monitored into the search bar and the result will be delivered on one page. You can use it to search multiple social platforms such as blogs, Facebook or Twitter either individually or all at the same time.

17. BackTweets

This tool tracks the number of people talking about you, identifies who is talking and what they're saying. It helps both individuals and companies measure their Twitter reach in quantity and quality by displaying how often a link was tweeted including the actual tweet that was made.

18. CustomScoop

This provides all-in-one news and social media monitoring. You can access different types of services, for instance a 24/7 automated dashboard or if your preference is a sophisticated human analysis you can get that too. CustomScoop provides customised solutions that will meet your needs.

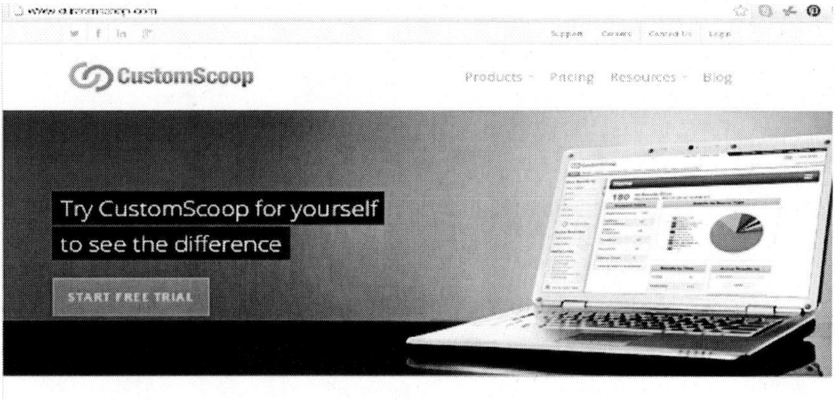

References

[1] http://socialmention.com/about/
[2] https://en.mention.com/features
[3]http://addictomatic.com/about

Conclusion

Oftentimes, businesses and organisations only take reputation management into consideration after something is already amiss – way after it's already too late to avoid the reputational damage.

The reputation of an organisation always precedes it and will open or close doors of opportunity before you ever get to the doors. The organisation's reputation is the lifeblood of the business, it takes a long time to establish but very little to destroy it. No matter how much an organisation advertises, it's the reputation that brings about the increase in sales and growth.

Even if everything is lost, ensure that the reputation is preserved as that is the one thing that should not be lost except of course if the reputation is bad.

With the growth of Social Media, it is of the utmost importance that an organisation's online reputation is managed effectively, as something as simple as one negative information online can have far-reaching repercussions.

Creating, preserving and enhancing a positive reputation online could be a deciding factor that contributes to your business making it or folding up. One negative remark about your organisation could send the business falling like a pack of cards.

An organisation's reputation is critical to its survival.

Summing it all up

We specialise in helping businesses get things set up to succeed online, and we're here, ready to help.

Take a look at our websites:

www.aceresultsmarketing.com

www.reputationmaven.com

Services We Can Offer

Online Reputation Management Services

We can help monitor, build, protect and repair your Business' reputation online.

SEO/First Page Google Service

We can help your business get found on the internet where people are looking: Google, Yahoo!, Bing, Ask, and other search engines. That means more potential visitors to your website, more phone calls, and more people physically walking through your door.

ADDITIONAL SERVICES WE PROVIDE

Mobile Marketing Mobile Websites Mobile Coupons Text Marketing Click To Call

Mobile Apps

On-Page Optimisation

Keyword Research Title Tag Optimisation
Image & Hyperlink Optimisation

Header Tag Optimization

Reporting

Website SEO audits

Google Analytics (Statistics)

Current Performance Monthly SEO Report

Local Search

Website Optimisation

Local Search Engine Submission

Customer Review Submission

Updating Pages for Local Search

Content Optimisation

Website Content Writing

Blog Writing Article Writing
Press Release Writing

Social Media Marketing

Video Marketing

Web 2.0 and Social Media Optimisation

Social Bookmarking

Blog Submission

Press Release Submission

Article Submission

PowerPoint Presentation Submission

Video Submission Photo Sharing RSS Feeds
Link Development

Manual Link Requests to Related Sites

One Way Links from Directory Submissions

Other Activities

Google, Yahoo & MSN Sitemap Creation

Made in United States
North Haven, CT
04 November 2026

21765290R00088